100 Great Wildlife Experiences

100 Great Wildlife Experiences

What to See and Where

James D. Fair

WHITE
OWL

First published in Great Britain in 2019 by
Pen and Sword White Owl
An imprint of
Pen & Sword Books Ltd
Yorkshire – Philadelphia

Copyright © James D Fair, 2019

Hardback ISBN 9781526723550
Paperback ISBN 9781526751560

Typeset in Palatino by Mac Style

Printed and bound in India by Replika Press Pvt. Ltd.

Pen & Sword Books Ltd incorporates the Imprints of Pen & Sword Books Archaeology, Atlas, Aviation, Battleground, Discovery, Family History, History, Maritime, Military, Naval, Politics, Railways, Select, Transport, True Crime, Fiction, Frontline Books, Leo Cooper, Praetorian Press, Seaforth Publishing, Wharncliffe and White Owl.

For a complete list of Pen & Sword titles please contact

PEN & SWORD BOOKS LIMITED
47 Church Street, Barnsley, South Yorkshire, S70 2AS, England
E-mail: enquiries@pen-and-sword.co.uk
Website: www.pen-and-sword.co.uk

or

PEN AND SWORD BOOKS
1950 Lawrence Rd, Havertown, PA 19083, USA
E-mail: Uspen-and-sword@casematepublishers.com
Website: www.penandswordbooks.com

CONTENTS

MAP KEY

1. Fishing white-tailed eagles, Loch na Keal, Isle of Mull
2. Basking sharks, Gunna Sound, Coll
3. Grey seals, Blakeney Point National Nature Reserve, Norfolk
4. Nightingales, Highnam Woods RSPB Reserve, Gloucestershire
5. Minke whales, North Sea (Staithes, Northumberland)
6. Pinkfooted geese, Snettisham RSPB Reserve, Norfolk
7. Northern gannets, Noss, Shetland
8. Red squirrels, Haweswater Hotel, Haweswater, Lake District National Park
9. Marsh harriers, Leighton Moss RSPB Reserve, Lancashire
10. Pine martens, Rothiemurchus Estate, Cairngorms National Park
11. Starling murmuration, Ham Wall RSPB Reserve, Somerset Levels
12. Common dolphins, Irish Sea (St Davids, Pembrokeshire Coast National Park)
13. Puffins, Hermaness National Nature Reserve, Unst, Shetland
14. Pipistrelle bats, Lacock Abbey, Wiltshire
15. Orcas, Shetland
16. Red kites, Bwlch Nant yr Arian, North Wales
17. Golden eagles, Isle of Harris, Outer Hebrides
18. Brown hares, Wallasea RSPB Reserve, Essex
19. Storm petrels, Mousa, Shetland
20. Otters, Shetland Mainland
21. Peregrine falcons, Norwich Cathedral, Norwich
22. Manx shearwaters, Skomer Island, Pembrokeshire Coast National Park
23. Red deer, Eastern Moors, Peak District National Park
24. Ospreys, Loch Garten RSPB Reserve, Cairngorms National Park
25. Swallowtail butterflies, Strumpshaw Fen RSPB Reserve, Norfolk
26. Cranes, Aller Moor, near Langport, Somerset Levels
27. Bottlenose dolphins, Cardigan Bay (New Quay), Ceredigion
28. Beavers, River Otter, Otterton, Devon
29. Glow-worms, Westbury-sub-Mendip, Somerset
30. (Swimming with) puffins, Skomer Island, Pembrokeshire Coast National Park
31. Dawn exodus, Ham Wall RSPB Reserve, Somerset Levels
32. Fulmars, Noup Cliffs RSPB Reserve, Westray, Orkney
33. Fossil hunting, Charmouth, Dorset
34. Greenshanks, Forsinard Flows RSPB Reserve, Caithness and Sutherland
35. Kestrels, Anywhere
36. Badgers, Nannerth Fawr Farm, Powys

37. Snake's head fritillaries, North Meadow National Nature Reserve, Wiltshire
38. Terns, Coquet Island RSPB Reserve (Amble), Northumberland
39. Ring-necked parakeets, Kensington Gardens, London
40. Common lizards, Cors Dyfi Nature Reserve, Powys, Wales
41. Arctic terns, Farne Islands (Seahouses), Northumberland
42. Wild boar, Forest of Dean, Gloucestershire
43. Orchids and other wildflowers, Clattinger Farm Nature Reserve, Wiltshire
44. Nightjars, Westleton Heath National Nature Reserve, Suffolk
45. Crabbing, New Quay, Ceredigion, Wales
46. Konik ponies, Wicken Fen National Nature Reserve, Cambridgeshire
47. Snorkel Trail, Kimmeridge Bay, Dorset
48. Barn owls, Lakenheath Fen RSPB Reserve, Suffolk
49. Willow warblers, Dunnet Head RSPB Reserve, Caithness and Sutherland
50. Camera-trapping, Anywhere
51. Seabird City, Shiant Isles, Outer Hebrides
52. Bluebells, Anywhere
53. Coal and crested tits, Loch Garten RSPB Reserve, Cairngorms National Park
54. Purple emperor butterflies, Knepp Estate, West Sussex
55. Marsh harriers and cranes, Hickling Broad National Nature Reserve, Norfolk
56. Hobbies, Shapwick Heath National Nature Reserve, Somerset Levels
57. Bitterns, Ham Wall RSPB Reserve, Somerset Levels
58. Sea kayaking, Dinas Head, Pembrokeshire Coast National Park
59. Portuguese man o' war, Portheras Cove, Cornwall
60. Reindeer, Glenmore, Cairngorms National Park
61. Kingfishers, Rye Meads RSPB Reserve, Hertfordshire
62. Great bustards, Salisbury Plain, Wiltshire
63. Bat detecting, Anywhere
64. Owl prowl, Anywhere
65. Basking adders, Humberhead Peatlands National Nature Reserve, South Yorkshire
66. Greater horseshoe bats, Buckfastleigh, Devon
67. Skylarks, Pewsey Downs National Nature Reserve, Wiltshire
68. Daffodils, Farndale, North York Moors National Park, North Yorkshire
69. Sika deer, Arne RSPB Reserve, Dorset
70. Choughs, Bardsey Island, Gwynedd, Wales
71. Great skuas, Hoy RSPB Reserve, Hoy, Orkney
72. Whooper swans, Welney Wetland Centre, Norfolk,
73. Rockpooling, North Landing, East Yorkshire
74. Lapwings, Westray, Orkney
75. Avocets, River Exe, (Topsham) Devon
76. Black grouse, Langdon Beck, Co Durham
77. Ravens, Brecon Beacons National Park, Wales
78. Goshawks, Forest of Dean, Gloucestershire

79. Ring ouzels, Dove Stone RSPB Reserve, Greater Manchester
80. Risso's dolphins, Bardsey Island, Gwynedd, Wales
81. White-beaked dolphins, North Sea (Seahouses), Northumberland
82. Sand martins, River Wye, Glasbury, Powys, Wales
83. Courting great crested grebes, Tring Reservoir, Hertfordshire
84. Patrolling dragonflies, Thursley Common, Surrey
85. Rasping corncrakes, Tiree, Inner Hebrides
86. Nesting swallows, Martin's Haven, Pembrokeshire Coast National Park
87. Spring and autumn migration, Spurn Point, East Yorkshire
88. Dissecting owl pellets, anywhere
89. Barnacle geese, Caerlaverock Wetland Centre, Dumfries and Galloway
90. Snowdrops, Snowdrop Valley, Wheddon Cross, Exmoor National Park
91. Eider ducks, Canna, Inner Hebrides
92. Screaming swifts, Oxford Museum of Natural History, Oxford
93. Leaping salmon, Philiphaugh Estate, Scottish Borders
94. Damselflies, Cors Caron National Nature Reserve, Ceredigion, Wales
95. Scottish wildcat safari, Ardnamurchan, Scottish Highlands
96. Breeding herons, Swell Wood RSPB Reserve, Somerset
97. Curlews, Walton Backwaters, Essex
98. Kittiwakes, Newcastle upon Tyne
99. Wild garlic, Woodchester Park, Gloucestershire
100. (Swimming with) blue sharks, Newquay, Cornwall

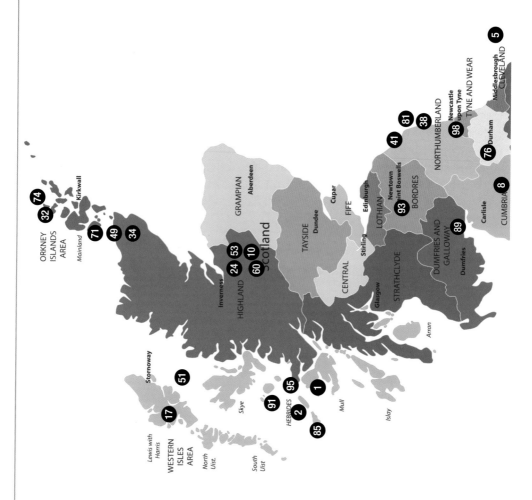

North Sea

North ATLANTIC OCEAN

ORKNEY ISLANDS AREA

Kirkwall

Mainland

GRAMPIAN

Aberdeen

Scotland

TAYSIDE

Dundee

Cupar

FIFE

CENTRAL

Stirling

Edinburgh

LOTHIAN

Newtown Saint Boswells

BORDRES

Glasgow

STRATHCLYDE

Arran

DUMFRIES AND GALLOWAY

Dumfries

NORTHUMBERLAND

Newcastle upon Tyne

TYNE AND WEAR

Durham

Carlisle

CUMBRIA

Middlesbrough

CLEVELAND

Inverness

HIGHLAND

Stornoway

Skye

HEBRIDES

Mull

Islay

Lewis with Harris

WESTERN ISLES AREA

North Uist.

South Uist

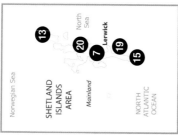

Norwegian Sea

North Sea

SHETLAND ISLANDS AREA

Mainland

Lerwick

NORTH ATLANTIC OCEAN

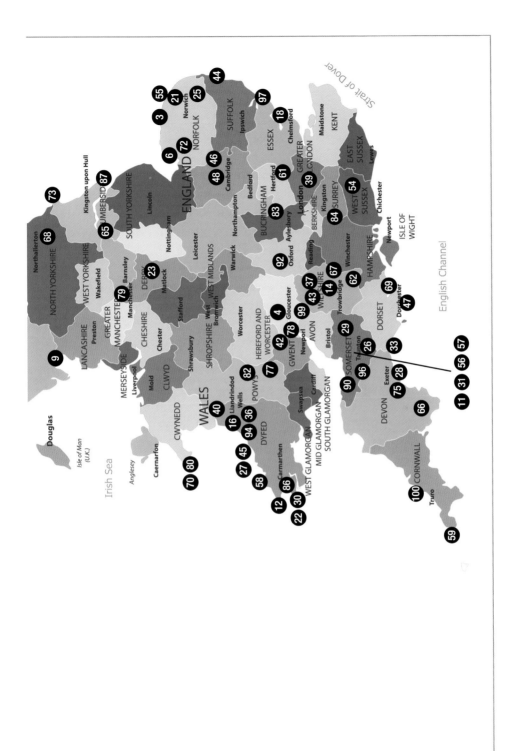

INTRODUCTION

Where in the world can you see the world's fastest animal (**Experience 21**), its second largest shark (**Experience 2**) and the oceans' top predator (**Experience 15**)? You can also visit a single location that is, for four or five months of the year, home to more than half of the entire population of one species of seabird – that's roughly 650,000 birds – (**Experience 22**), or, in a Scottish sea loch, come face-to-beak with one of Europe's largest birds of prey (**Experience 1**).

Oh, it also has half the entire global population of a much-loved wildflower (**Experience 52**), and a beetle that thinks it's a fly or even a worm (**Experience 29**). And that's not forgetting a rodent that can fell trees, re-engineer landscapes and is the largest to be found anywhere outside of the Americas (**Experience 28**).

WHERE IN THE WORLD? YES, GREAT BRITAIN, OF COURSE.

And that's without even mentioning the puffins, pine martens, parakeets, pinkfooted geese, pipistrelle bats and – for those who like just a smidgeon of danger in their lives – Portuguese men o'war that can all be found here, mostly with little difficulty and relatively little expense. You won't have to fork out any huge airfares or national park fees to go on safari here, though it is true that for some experiences, you may have to beef up your winter wardrobe. Take it from me, it can get mighty cold on the North Norfolk coast in December.

It bears repeating that Britain is an island and a coastal nation, and while it doesn't have the great diversity of fauna of an African savannah or tropical rainforest, it does possess rich marine resources on which an abundance of birds, sharks and marine mammals, including bottlenose dolphins (**Experience 27**) and minke whales (**Experience 5**), feed. These islands are home to 40 per cent of the planet's grey seals (**Experience 3**), and with 300,000 pairs, about 55 per cent of all Northern gannets (**Experience 7**), the North Atlantic's largest seabird. It's no coincidence that more than a third (35 out of 100) of the wildlife experiences I've compiled put you either by, on or even in the sea (**Experiences 2, 30, 47 and 100**).

Part of my motivation for writing this book was to demonstrate that many great wildlife experiences in Britain are accessible to even quite young children. My number one experience – watching white-tailed eagles taking fish from the waters of Loch na Keal on the isle of Mull – was something I did with my partner and then six and three-year-old sons, who were equally if not more mesmerised by the 'flying barn doors' as we were. We've also taken them on bottlenose dolphin cruises (**Experience 27**) in Cardigan Bay, to a starling murmuration (**Experience 11**) in the Somerset Levels, fossil hunting (**Experience 33**) on Dorset's Jurassic Coast, on a wild boar hunt (**Experience 42**) in Gloucestershire and to watch plunge-diving terns off Coquet Island (**Experience 38**) in the North Sea – and they've enjoyed them all. Well, most of them.

There are a few things that are worth bearing in mind before you set out on any wildlife adventures. I would like to make the following five points:

➡ Apart from having the appropriate clothes for the weather and conditions you are likely to face, especially if you're taking children, the most important item you need is a pair of binoculars. These days, you can get a perfectly decent pair for £100-200. Don't be seduced by those teeny travel binoculars, they're not worth the money, and don't just shop online for them – visit a decent optical retailer and get some good advice. Minox, Opticron and Viking are all good brands at the cheaper end of the scale, but go with whatever works for you.

➡ With a few exceptions, for each experience listed, I've named one main location, and unless otherwise indicated, getting there is just a question of putting the postcode of the reserve into your SatNav or smartphone. In the 'Do it yourself' section at the end of the entry, where possible (which is in most but not every case), I've added other places you can try for the same species, but I may not have first-hand knowledge of these locations.

➡ Apart from where an experience is, it's equally important to take account of when it takes place. Most are seasonal – in many cases, they relate to migrant birds, such as swallows, that come here for the spring or many others that overwinter here, fleeing even colder climes to the north and east. Or they may relate to behaviour, such as the red (**Experience 23**) and sika (**Experience 69**) deer ruts.

➡ There's a star rating system for each experience based on whether it's family friendly (ie, suitable for and appealing to children), budget friendly (how much it will cost) and amateur friendly (how much expertise you require). Any experiences that required very high levels of knowledge, identification skills or fieldcraft haven't been included.

➡ Finally, there are lots of books that help you identify British wildlife but, in my view, the most important thing by far is a field guide to British birds.

So, what are you waiting for? There's a whole world – well, OK, small, windswept, often wet, sometimes cold, very occasionally warm island – of wildlife out there to explore.

James can be contacted via his website (www.jamesfairwildlife.co.uk) or on Twitter (@jamesfairwild).

100 SWIMMING WITH BLUE SHARKS

Family friendly ★
Blue sharks aren't dangerous, but this is for confident snorkelers only

Budget friendly ★
A day out may cost up to £250

Amateur friendly ★ ★ ★
Ability to snorkel essential

Best time of year
August

B lue sharks are a caricature of how you might draw a shark – a comically pointy nose, a mouth shaped into a downward grimace, big eyes and an outsized tail. But at the same time, they're stunning to look at, their top sides a shimmering azure blue, a colour I don't think I've ever seen on another living animal.

Cage-diving with blue sharks, which are fairly common in British waters, began off Cornwall about ten years or so ago, and now there are a few operators doing variations on this theme. If you think the cage is for lightweights, you can also go snorkelling with them in open water. Blue sharks aren't regarded as dangerous to people, though I can't claim first-hand knowledge of this.

Trips take up to a whole day, and sharks are lured to the boat with mashed-up fish remains known as chum. Not for the faint-hearted.

DO IT YOURSELF

Charles Hood Photography does snorkelling with blue sharks without a cage.
⌾ charleshood.com ☎ 07712 622440

Newquay Safaris does cage-diving trips from June to September.
⌾ www.newquayseasafarisandfishing.co.uk ☎ 01637 877613

99 WILD GARLIC

WOODCHESTER PARK, NEAR STROUD

Family friendly ★★★★★
Woodchester Park is stunning location with a fabulous play trail for children

Budget friendly ★★★★
A small car parking charge

Amateur friendly ★★★★★
Wild garlic's a doddle to identify

Best time of year
March-late April

Toilets ✓
Cafe ✓
(Only open Friday-Sunday from late March)

I grew up in the South-east, and it wasn't until I was in my early 20s that I recall seeing the vast, creamy-white drifts of wild garlic that you find in the South-west. Here, this fabulous spring spectacle is so ubiquitous it's faintly absurd to recommend a single place – any relatively mature woodland is likely to provide good habitat. From a distance, the flowers merge into a single frothy layer like the top of a cappuccino, but close-up, they are delicate six-petalled flowers with equally delicate stamens poking out like an insect's antennae. The drifts of wild garlic in Woodchester Park, which is worth a visit at any time of year for the unfinished gothic mansion, are particularly special and extensive – the best ones are at the eastern end of the park below the mansion.

DO IT YOURSELF

Woodchester Park (GL10 3TS) is south of Stroud, just off the B4066 near Nympsfield. Don't go to the village of Woodchester – it's at the wrong end of the park from the car park.
🖱 www.nationaltrust.org.uk/woodchester-park ☎ 01452 814213

BBC Countryfile Magazine has some great ideas for other wild garlic destinations.
🖱 www.countryfile.com/wild-garlic-guide-plus-recipes

98 SCREECHING KITTIWAKES

NEWCASTLE QUAYSIDE

Family friendly ★★★★★
Get an ice cream while you're at it

Budget friendly ★★★★★
Apart from the ice creams

Amateur friendly ★★★★
Listen out for 'Kittiwake! Kittiwake!'

Best time of year
April-July

Kittiwakes are gulls, like those you see in seaside resorts, but they are smaller, prettier birds and they are only found onshore during the breeding season. The rest of the time, they are far out at sea, as far afield as the coasts of Mexico or West Africa.

They usually nest on isolated cliff-faces, but for some reason, hundreds of pairs have taken up residence on the quayside in the heart of Newcastle upon Tyne, with many nesting on or around the mighty Tyne Bridge. Their call is an ear-piercing, three-syllable sound that just about sounds like 'Kittiwake! Kittiwake!'

They are colonial nesters, so where you get one, you get hundreds or even thousands. In the Norwegian archipelago of Svalbard, I once visited a colony of 10,000 or more, so look on this as a taste of the Arctic in one of Britain's greatest cities.

DO IT YOURSELF

Watch them from anywhere around the Tyne Bridge, from the viewing area on the fourth floor of the Baltic Art Gallery and from the Kittiwake Tower downstream from the Baltic.

The Natural History Society of Northumbria has more information.
🖰 www.nhsn.ncl.ac.uk/activities/conservation-research/tyne-kittiwakes ☎ 0191 208 2790

97 BURBLING CURLEWS

WALTON BACKWATERS (HAMFORD WATER)

Family friendly ★★★
Children will enjoy the boat trip

Budget friendly ★★
A boat trip will cost more than
£40 for a family of four

Amateur friendly ★★★★★
The haunting call is
unmistakeable

Best time of year
More birds in estuaries during
the winter

I spent many happy holidays when I was young messing about on Essex's River Blackwater, so I have soft spot for the county others mainly associate with nail and tanning salons. In my mind's eye, I go back to the Walton Backwaters – immortalised by Arthur Ransome in Secret Water – and I'm sitting on boat as the sun sets, surrounded by tidal creeks, mud banks and saltmarsh. Somewhere out of sight, a curlew starts to call, a burbling sound rising like a bubble of gas that's lighter than air. I might even see one, stalking along the tide line, that gently downward-curving bill probing the mud for crustaceans or worms.

DO IT YOURSELF

Walk around the southern side of the Backwaters via the seawall or take a boat trip. ✆ www.walton-on-the-naze.com/wildlife-boat-trips/ ☎ 07806 309460

You can visit Skipper's Island, a small wildlife reserve owned by Essex Wildlife Trust. Access by appointment only. ✆ www.essexwt.org.uk/reserves/skippers-island ☎ 01621 862960

Curlews are common in many of our estuaries during the winter, and breed in upland areas such as North Wales, the Pennines and many parts of Scotland.

96 BREEDING HERONS

SWELL WOOD RSPB RESERVE

Family friendly ★★★
Children might enjoy this
unusual bird-watching
experience

Budget friendly ★★★★★
The reserve is free

Amateur friendly ★★★★★
There's nothing like a heron

Best time of year
March-April

I bet most of the times you've seen a heron, they've been standing silent and motionless in a river or lake as if frozen in time, or perhaps flying overhead like modern-day pterosaurs. But during the breeding season, they become gregarious and noisy birds. They nest in woods, and there are places in Britain where you can have up to 150 pairs in a colonial heronry.

Swell Wood, overlooking the Somerset Levels, usually has about 80 pairs, but what makes it unique is the hide. Instead of being hunched up in a small, dark room with windows like portholes, you are in the open air sitting on benches that tilt backwards, so that you can – quite literally – sit back and enjoy the view.

DO IT YOURSELF

Swell Wood (TA3 6PX) is at the southern edge of the Somerset Levels.
🖱 www.rspb.org/swellwood ☎ 01458 252805

There is a heronry of about 30 nests in Battersea Park, London. The Wildlife Trusts have more information on places to go on their website.
🖱 www.wildlifetrusts.org/where_to_see_a_heronry

95 SCOTTISH WILDCAT SAFARI

ARDNAMURCHAN PENINSULA

Family friendly ★
Late night sorties in search of one of Britain's most elusive mammals

Budget friendly ★★★

Amateur friendly ★
Can be hard to tell the difference between a wildcat and a feral domestic moggie

Best time of year
All year round

Though wildcats are the ancestors of domestic ones and look superficially like the tabby in your living room, that's as far as it goes. First, they're bigger animals, with a head and body length of up to 75cm – try measuring your family pet for comparison – and can weigh anywhere between 3-6kg.

And second, people who have studied them report they're about as far removed from wanting to curl up on a sofa as an Amazonian jaguar would be – they're not called wildcats for nothing. They used to be found throughout Britain, but persecution and habitat loss has meant they are now restricted to a few, remote areas of Scotland. A further problem is they can breed and produce fertile young with domestic cats, leading to impure hybrids resembling the original species.

DO IT YOURSELF

Wild Highland Tours offers day, dusk and night-time safaris from its base at Glenborrowdale, on the north side of Loch Sunart. You're most likely to see badgers, foxes, owls and deer – count any wildcat sighting as a bonus. 🖰 www.wildhighlandtours.co.uk ☎ 01972 500742

94 DAMSELFLIES

CORS CARON NATIONAL NATURE RESERVE, TREGARON

Family friendly ★★★★
Easy walking on a boardwalk

Budget friendly ★★★★★
Even the car park is free

Amateur friendly ★★★★★
Easy to spot and recognise

Best time of year
May-August

Toilets ✓

According to the British Dragonfly Society, 24 species of dragonfly and damselfly can be found at Cors Caron, including some real beauties such as the emperor dragonfly and southern hawker, but what I love is the sheer number of blue damselflies you can see here – yes, these are common insects that you could even see in your back garden or local park, but I've never been anywhere else where they gathered in such profusion.

There's a boardwalk that's perfect for the very young or old, and from May onwards (pick a warm, calm day if possible), these stunning, powder-blue bog beasts are everywhere in quantities almost impossible to fathom. Even if you only stop for half an hour, it will be a memorable experience.

DO IT YOURSELF

Cors Caron NNR (SY25 6JF) is very easy to find – it's on the B4343 less than two miles north of Tregaron. ⁂ naturalresources.wales/days-out/places-to-visit/mid-wales/cors-caron-national-nature-reserve/?lang=en ☎ 0300 065 3000

The British Dragonfly Society has recommendations for other locations for damselflies and dragonflies. ⁂ british-dragonflies.org.uk/content/where-see-dragonflies

93 LEAPING SALMON

PHILLIPHAUGH ESTATE, SELKIRK

Family friendly ★★★
Educational displays about the salmon's life cycle

Budget friendly ★★★★★
The salmon viewing centre has free entry

Amateur friendly ★★★★★

Best time of year
Sept-Nov

Toilets ✓
Cafe ✓

The migration of Atlantic salmon upriver to mate, reproduce and ensure the ongoing survival of the species is the saddest of journeys. They are exhausted by its rigours and cannot feed (so gradually get thinner and thinner), while males are engaged in constant conflict with others as they earn their right to mate with females.

By the time they have spawned, most are so thin they succumb to predators or disease (and that's without mentioning the fly fishermen looking to snag a 15 pounder). Not only that, but natural and artificial obstacles, from waterfalls to weirs, stand in their way as they push upriver to the higher reaches where females will lay their eggs.

DO IT YOURSELF

The Philliphaugh Estate has a salmon viewing centre, which explains more about the salmon's lifecycle and has cameras with live feeds. You can watch salmon for yourself at The Cauld. The best time of year to go is October and November, and salmon are more active after heavy rain. It's 1 mile to the south-west of Selkirk on the A708. ⌐ www.salmonviewingcentre.com ☎ 01750 21766

Leaping salmon can also be seen just outside the village of Stainforth in North Yorkshire.
⌐ www.visitsettle.co.uk/stainforth-force.html

92 SCREAMING SWIFTS

OXFORD MUSEUM OF NATURAL HISTORY

Family friendly ★★
Swifts fly very high, making it difficult for children

Budget friendly ★★★★★
Swift-watching is free

Amateur friendly ★★★
People confuse swifts with swallows, so learn to tell them apart

Best time of year
May–August

Toilets ✓
Cafe ✓

The swifts' sojourn in Britain is brief indeed. Traditionally, they arrive here on 1 May and leave in the first week of August, a stay of just over three months. They're one of the few migrant birds that are happy to breed in cities, and they nest in loose colonies of dozens of pairs.

Swifts may look superficially like swallows, but they're quite different. They're larger and fly with stiff wing beats then soar on sickle-shaped wings. Groups of swifts often fly together in close formation emitting high-pitched screams, and according to Edward Mayer, of Swift Conservation, we don't fully understand the reason for this behaviour, though there appears to be some kind of social purpose.

DO IT YOURSELF

Oxford Museum of Natural History (OX1 3PW) has a swifts nesting in its tower – about 24 active nests in 2017. The museum has installed cameras in some of the nest boxes, and footage can be watched online. ⌕ www.oum.ox.ac.uk/learning/htmls/swifts.htm ☎ 01865 272 950

Other places recommended by Swift Conservation include the Chantry House in Henley-on-Thames, Gayton Crescent in Hampstead and Hastings old town.

91 EIDER DUCKS

CANNA, INNER HEBRIDES

Family friendly ★★★★
Children love ducks, especially ones which make strange calls

Budget friendly ★★★
Yes – but they tend to live in remote places

Amateur friendly ★★★★★
Easy to recognise

Best time of year
April-Sept

With their glossy black and white plumage, and not forgetting the eccentric dab of mustard yellow at the back of the neck, male eider ducks really are handsome creatures (the females, alas, like so many other ducks, are brown and speckled). They also do a remarkably good impression of the late comedian Frankie Howerd. 'Ooooh! Ooooh!' they chant as if they've just heard a particularly saucy *double entendre*. 'I don't mind if I do.'

In Britain, eider ducks are mainly found around the coast of Scotland, though I've seen them in the harbour at Sea Houses in Northumberland. Eider ducks will also breed as far north as Svalbard in the High Arctic, hence the necessity for those warm, soft feathers from which we get eiderdown and which females pluck from their breast to line the nest.

DO IT YOURSELF

You don't have to travel all the way to Canna to see eider ducks, but in the peace of the small harbour, it is a particularly special experience. Ferries leave from Mallaig on the mainland.
⌂ www.calmac.co.uk/destinations/canna   ☎ 0800 066 5000

90 SNOWDROPS

SNOWDROP VALLEY, EXMOOR

Family friendly ★★★

Budget friendly ★★★★★
Nothing to pay

Amateur friendly ★★★★★
Everyone knows a snowdrop

Best time of year
Jan-Feb

Appearing as they do in mid-to-late January, in what is frequently the coldest time of year, snowdrops feel more like a mid-winter miracle than the first signs of spring. Still, where they carpet a forest floor, producing a distinctive white and green appearance, they are an undeniably beautiful sight.

Anyone with access to decent woodlands or even city parks can see snowdrops, but for a wildflower experience like no other, it's hard to beat Snowdrop Valley on Exmoor. It's actually a part of the Avill Valley, just to the north of the village of Wheddon Cross, and though it's privately owned, a few walking routes are opened up in late January and February every year so that anyone can enjoy the show.

DO IT YOURSELF

Snowdrop Valley is owned by the Badgworthy Land Company – the parish council of Wheddon Cross & Cutcombe helped negotiate access and lays on transport from Wheddon Cross to the valley. Exmoor National Park has more information. ⌂ www.exmoor-nationalpark.gov.uk/enjoying/events ☎ 01398 323665

There's also information and maps showing three walking trails (all likely to be rough and muddy) on the parish council's website. ⌂ www.wheddoncross.org.uk/snowdropvalley.htm

89 BARNACLE GEESE

WWT CAERLAVEROCK, SOLWAY FIRTH

Family friendly ★★★★
Most WWT reserves are very child friendly

Budget friendly ★★
Will cost just over £20 for a family of four, free to members

Amateur friendly ★★★
Beautiful, highly distinctive geese

Best time of year
Dec-March

Toilets ✓
Cafe ✓

In the 1940s, the barnacle goose population at the Wildfowl and Wetlands Trust (WWT) Caerlaverock reserve had sunk to just a few hundred animals. Today, thanks in part to habitat restoration work, some 35,000 gather here for the winter, a welcome antidote to the seemingly endless decline of our wildlife elsewhere. The geese overwinter here, arriving in early October and staying until March – they're beautiful birds, too, with an unmistakeable, monochrome plumage.

Caerlaverock has four observation towers, four observatories and 20 smaller hides from which to watch the spectacle. It also has a farmhouse where you can stay the night in to get the best of the early morning and late evening action.

DO IT YOURSELF

WWT Caerlaverock (DG1 4RS) is on the Solway Firth, 25km west of Gretna Green. Apart from the barnacle geese, winter highlights include daily feeding of thousands of wild whooper swans.
🖱 www.wwt.org.uk/wetland-centres/caerlaverock ☎ 01387 770200

Loch Gruinart RSPB Reserve (PA44 7PP) on Islay also has barnacle geese in the winter.
🖱 www.rspb.org/lochgruinart ☎ 01496 850505

88 DISSECTING OWL PELLETS

Family friendly ★★★★
Children will love to be nature detectives

Budget friendly ★★★★★
You need a bowl of water, some forceps and the pellets

Amateur friendly ★★★
Dissecting the owl pellet isn't difficult – finding them may be

Best time of year
All year round

Almost as soon as I dunked the dark pellets into the water, they started to come apart. A couple of them were quite fresh, so still soft and squidgy, and soon skulls and sliver-thin limb bones began to materialise. Careful probing with the tweezers, poking the dark matter of the pellet from out of eye sockets and from within the jaws neatly finished the job. The skulls are the pellets' real jewels – tiny, delicate remains of an owl's meal that it egests through its mouth within the pellet. Close examination of them, and in particular the tooth-root pattern, will tell you exactly which rodent species they belong to.

DO IT YOURSELF

The Barn Owl Trust's tells you how to identify skull remains. ⌁ www.barnowltrust.org.uk/barn-owl-facts/barn-owl-pellet-analysis; the RSPB also has useful tips on how to dissect owl pellets. ⌁ ww2.rspb.org.uk/Images/Owlpellets_tcm9-133500.pdf

To find owl pellets, see if you can work out where owls in your area roost. Farmers or landowners may have owls on their land, ask if you can look for roosting spots.

87 SPRING AND AUTUMN MIGRATION

SPURN POINT

Family friendly ★★★
Migrant birds might not interest children, but the lighthouse might

Budget friendly ★★★★
The carpark costs £4

Amateur friendly ★★
Yes, but swot up on your bird ID

Best time of year
April-May and Sept-Oct

Toilets ✓
Cafe ✓

Many migrant birds use outlying bits of our coast as refuelling spots either on their way north in the spring or on their way south in the autumn, and they can gather in these places in their tens of thousands, making for a remarkable spectacle.

Spurn Point is one such place. A finger of sand and gravel extending into the Humber Estuary, it is an other-worldly place, and it provides food and shelter for many birds making their way up or down the North Sea or coming across from mainland Europe. My only visit to Spurn in migration season coincided with gale force, Arctic winds blowing, and we barely saw a bird all day, so perhaps look at a weather forecast before you go.

DO IT YOURSELF

Yorkshire Wildlife Trust runs 'Spurn Safaris', which cost £14 for adults, £7 for children (2018 prices).
🖱 www.ywt.org.uk/nature-reserves/spurn-national-nature-reserve   ☎ 01964 650144

A migration festival is held every autumn at Spurn Point (HU12 0UH).
🖱 www.spurnmigfest.com

Other good places to see the migration in full swing include Flamborough Head, Fair Isle, Bardsey Island, the Scilly Isles and Portland Bill.

86 NESTING SWALLOWS

MARTIN'S HAVEN

Family friendly ★★★★★
They're in the toilets!

Budget friendly ★★★★★
No charge – even for the toilets

Amateur friendly ★★★★★
Easy to spot

Best time of year
May-July

You have to be careful watching nesting birds not to disturb them, but there is a place where you can safely see them flying in and out with food for their chicks and their gape-mouthed offspring. Given that these birds breed in this location every year, and hundreds of people walk in and out of it most days, they clearly don't find our presence off-putting.

It's the toilets at Martin's Haven in Pembrokeshire, just outside Marloes (you catch the boat to Skomer here). I've been going there with my partner (and more recently two children) for at least ten years, and I can't think of a single occasion during the spring or summer when I haven't seen swallows nesting here. The coastal grasslands must provide plenty of insect fodder, while the basic toilet block provides the shelter they need – even if they do have to put up with some funny smells.

DO IT YOURSELF

Martin's Haven is about 3km out of Marloes. There is a National Trust carpark here (free to members), and it's a minute or two's walk to the toilet block. The Wildlife Trust of South and West Wales has a small shop here, too.

85 RASPING CORNCRAKES

TIREE, INNER HEBRIDES

Family friendly ★★★
Possibly not the corncrakes, but Tiree is a beautiful island with beaches to die for

Budget friendly ★★★
Free experience, but a remote location

Amateur friendly ★★★★
Do some swotting up on the corncrake's call

Best time of year
May-June

© John Bowler.

Tiree is surely the most beautiful place name in Britain, redolent of the island's exotic white sandy beaches (it's been nicknamed the 'Hawaii of the north') and wind-swept nature. I've only been there once; it was for just a few hours, it was at the wrong time of year for corncrakes and an apocalyptic autumnal gale was building to a crescendo – still, it was worth it.

Corncrakes only come to the UK from Africa for the breeding season. They're extremely hard to see (I've only heard them), but like many birds, they are renowned for how they sound – in this case, a rasping noise that's been compared to someone running their fingers down a plastic comb or playing the washboard at high speed.

They're found on other islands in the Inner and Outer Hebrides, but Tiree has one third of the entire UK breeding population of about 900 pairs.

DO IT YOURSELF

Ferries to Tiree depart from Oban.
🖱 www.calmac.co.uk/destinations/tiree   ☎ 0800 066 5000

There's more information about Tiree's birds and other wildlife here:
🖱 www.isleoftiree.com/island-diary/bird-news   ☎ 01879 220748

84 PATROLLING DRAGONFLIES

THURSLEY COMMON

Family friendly ★★★
Some children will find dragonflies fun, others may not

Budget friendly ★★★★★
A cheap day out, if nothing else

Amateur friendly ★★★★★
Everyone knows what a dragonfly is

Best time of year
July-August

In films about dystopian futures, there are frequently drone-like machines that spy on the populace for the authoritarian regime. Any close examination of these spybots would surely reveal they have been modelled on dragonflies.

It's not just those absurdly big eyes that look as if they must be able to look in 60 directions at once or could have been the inspiration for a virtual reality headset, or indeed those outsized tails that make them resemble super-fast torpedoes – no, it's the way they move, the impression they give that they are being remotely controlled by a gamer in their bedsit.

While hawkers are the biggest and most impressive of our dragonflies, keep an eye out too for the smaller, stubbier chasers and darters.

DO IT YOURSELF

Thursley Common (GU8 6LW) is a National Nature Reserve located between the villages of Elstead and Thursley, south of Guildford in Surrey. Park at the Moat car park. ⌐ www.gov.uk/government/publications/surreys-national-nature-reserves/surreys-national-nature-reserves

Learn to identify your dragonflies using the British Dragonfly Society's website.
⌐ british-dragonflies.org.uk

83 COURTING GREAT CRESTED GREBES

TRING RESERVOIRS

Family friendly ★★
I'm not sure children will be interested in dancing water birds

Budget friendly ★★★★★
This one's free

Amateur friendly ★★★
Great crested grebes are one of our most easily recognisable water birds

Best time of year
Late Feb-June

With their punk hair-dos and elaborate collars on long, slim elegant necks, great crested grebes are very easily recognisable and beautiful water birds. To me, they seem almost impossibly exotic for this country, especially when you see them on something as mundane and prosaic as a reservoir. They should be found in a location far more refined than Tring!

And then there's their courtship dance, the culmination of which sees the male and the female rising out of the water and presenting each other with weed from the bottom of the lake or reservoir.

DO IT YOURSELF

For more information about Tring Reservoirs (HP23 4PA), Herts and Middlesex Wildlife Trust
✆ www.hertswildlifetrust.org.uk/nature-reserves/tring-reservoirs ☎ 01727 858901

Other good spots include Windsor Great Park, in Berks (www.royal-windsor.com), Cotswold Water Park, in Gloucestershire and Wiltshire (✆ www.waterpark.org/cwp-trust) and Lake Vyrnwy (SY10 0LZ), in Powys (✆ www.rspb.org.uk/lakevyrnwy).

COURTING GREAT CRESTED GREBES

82 CANOEING WITH SAND MARTINS

RIVER WYE, GLASBURY

Family friendly ★★★★
Most children will love
canoeing down the Wye

Budget friendly ★★
Expect to pay up to £60-80
for half a day's canoeing for a
family of four

Amateur friendly ★★★
Easy to spot the sand martins

Best time of year
April-June

Sand martins are the less well-known siblings of swallows and house martins, and like them, after over-wintering thousands of miles away in sub-Saharan Africa, they return to Europe to breed. Sand martins differ in being found exclusively close to freshwater rivers and lakes, where they feed.

Watching them hawk for insects from the riverbank can be fun, but for a more immersive experience, try taking to the water. As you drift gently down the river in a canoe, you'll find them zipping all around you, hoovering up insects on the wing. Look out, too, for them returning to the tunnels in the riverbanks where they nest and bring up their chicks.

DO IT YOURSELF

Open canoes can be hired at Wye Valley Canoes (HR3 5NP) in Glasbury, with a choice of half-day, all-day or two-day trips. ⌨ www.wyevalleycanoes.co.uk ☎ 01497 847007

Cotswold Water Park also has sand martins. Lake 16 (just south of South Cerney) is often a good place to see them. CWP Trust ⌨ www.waterpark.org/cwp-trust ☎ 01793 752413

81 WHITE-BEAKED DOLPHINS

SEAHOUSES

Family friendly ★
4-5 hours at sea in potentially rough weather

Budget friendly ★★
Costs £65 (2017 price) for an adult

Amateur friendly ★★★
You'll have an expert to spot and identify dolphins

Best time of year
June-August

© Ben Burville.

Most Brits probably don't even know of the existence of white-beaked dolphins. Unlike bottlenose dolphins (**Experience 27**), they are more pelagic in their nature, preferring offshore, deeper waters, and in comparison to common dolphins (**Experience 12**), they are more at home in colder temperatures.

But an encounter with these playful marine mammals can be every bit as – if not more – exhilarating as with these other dolphins. They are fast, agile animals and love to bow-ride in the pressure wave at the front of a fast boat. This may reduce their own energy expenditure (a bit like a cyclist riding in the slipstream of another, but in reverse), but it could just be fun.

DO IT YOURSELF

North Sea Pelagics offers dedicated trips to find white-beaked dolphins in the North Sea. Trips leave from Seahouses.
🖱 www.northseapelagics.co.uk   ☎ 07932 577608 (Ben Burville) – they would probably not take children younger than 9 or 10.

White-beaked dolphins are also seen in Lyme Bay, off the coast of Dorset. Naturetrek
🖱 www.naturetrek.co.uk/tours/seabirds-and-cetaceans-of-lyme-bay   ☎ 01962 733051

80 RISSO'S DOLPHINS

BARDSEY ISLAND

Family friendly ★
A difficult species to see, and there are few home comforts on Bardsey

Budget friendly ★★★
You can get to, and stay on, Bardsey relatively cheaply

Amateur friendly ★
If you get a good look at a Risso's dolphin, they are very distinctive – you just need to get a good look

Best time of year
August-Sept

Toilets ✓
Self-catering kitchen and store ✓

© Peter Evans/Sea Watch Foundation.

My first sighting of a Risso's dolphin was off the island of Pico, in the Azores – after a few days watching mainly sperm whales, we came across a pod of six or seven Risso's late one afternoon. They are strange, dark-grey beasts that are easily identified by the white scarring all over their bodies that is said to be the result of tooth scrapes from other dolphins, as well as their prominent, sickle-shaped dorsal fins.

Though looking nothing like sperm whales, they have similar tastes in cephalopods – squid and octopus – so the deep waters off the Azores are a

DO IT YOURSELF

Bardsey Lodge and Bird Observatory is a cheap but basic option for staying on the island. It's self-catering (you have to bring all your fresh food to the island, but tins and dried foods can be bought there), and usually you have to stay for a whole week. ☝ www.bbfo.org.uk ☎ 01626 773908

More information from the Bardsey Island Trust, which has a number of self-catering cottages to rent out. ☝ www.bardsey.org ☎ 08458 112233

The north and west of Anglesey, and the Outer Hebrides, may also provide sightings of Risso's dolphins.

hotspot for both species. A few years later, I discovered these exotic dolphins can also be found off the British coast, albeit in smaller numbers and much harder to see. Still, I wanted to have a go.

So, I travelled up to Bardsey, also renowned for its choughs (**Experience 70**), where the wildlife group Whale and Dolphin Conservation (WDC) monitors for sightings of Risso's for six weeks during August and September.

WDC's Pine Eisfeld showed me pictures she'd taken the previous year of a pod of ten or twelve Risso's dolphins cavorting around their boat just off the island. It looked incredible, but I knew that Risso's dolphins can't be relied upon to behave like this with any certainty.

And so it proved. After spotting a small pod some distance out to sea from the island's bird observatory – I caught brief glimpses of a few dorsal fins and those strangely scarred, ghostly grey bodies – we saw no more for the next three days, just migrating skuas and other seabirds, plus the resident seals that were starting to pup, and some porpoises on my last morning.

In short, I'd only recommend this if you value the thrill of the chase more than the satisfaction of cornering of your quarry. It would seem Risso's dolphins – at least here in Britain – have no desire to become nailed-down wildlife sightings.

79 RING OUZELS

DOVE STONE RSPB RESERVE

Family friendly ★
A small black bird that you're unlikely to see close up

Budget friendly ★★★★
Free to see – though an expensive spotting scope would be useful

Amateur friendly ★
A lot of expertise required

Best time of year
April-July

Toilets ✓
(Mobile) Cafe ✓

The ring ouzel is a small, dark bird often called the mountain blackbird, and indeed it differs little from its much commoner, better-known relative, its main distinguishing feature being a crescent-shaped white bib on its chest which leaves the impression it's just about to tuck into a particularly hearty but potentially messy banquet.

It's rare too, especially in England, where there are proportionately fewer upland areas (compared with Scotland and Wales) that it requires, and those that do exist have been damaged by overgrazing. The British Trust for Ornithology estimates there are around 5,300 pairs in total in the UK.

So, what's the big deal? The truth is, I'm not a compulsive 'ticker' of new bird species, but when in April of 2017 I set out on a cycle ride from the south

DO IT YOURSELF

Dove Stone RSPB Reserve (closest postcode OL3 7NE) is on the north-east side of Greater Manchester, and about a 20-30 minute walk from Greenfield train station.
✍ www.rspb.org/dovestone ☎ 01457 819880

The Highlands of Scotland, North Pennines, Snowdonia and Brecon Beacons also have ring ouzels, and they're found as far south as Dartmoor.

of England to the north of Scotland, theoretically following spring north, one of the species I was determined to see was a ring ouzel.

It's not a traditional icon of spring, like the swallow, but along with countless other migrants from Africa, its arrival suggests something's in the air. But here's what I really admire about the ring ouzel: on reaching our shores, instead of heading to a nice, warm lowland wood or wetland like most of our other migrants, it decides to raise a family in some of the coldest and most godforsaken parts of the country.

Like Dove Stone. On the day I arrived in late April, it had been a bitterly cold morning and my feet were as frozen as two blocks of ice, and it took all the restorative powers of a hot Vimto – a northern cultural phenomenon I had been blissfully unaware of until then – at the mobile café to thaw me out. I was meeting the warden, the aptly named Jon Bird, and I'd made it clear in advance what my goal was.

Up at Chew Reservoir, more than 200 metres above the valley floor, it started snowing, and things weren't looking good for me and the ring ouzel. But as we were coming back down, Jon spotted something moving about on the boulder scree some 200m away. He whipped out his spotting scope with superhuman speed and soon located my first-ever mountain blackbird, clearly identifiable by that natty white bib. I've never been so pleased to see a small bird in all my life.

78 SKYDANCING GOSHAWKS

FOREST OF DEAN, GLOUCESTERSHIRE

Family friendly ★
Requires patience and good eyesight – not one for children

Budget friendly ★★★★
Free – unless you pay for an expert guide and increase your chances of seeing one

Amateur friendly ★
From a distance, it's not easy to distinguish goshawks from other birds of prey

Best time of year
March

Among serious wildlife enthusiasts and birders, the goshawk is one of our most revered birds of prey. This reverence is earned for a number of reasons – first, they cannot resist an animal that's both rare and elusive. The goshawk is the larger cousin to the much commoner sparrowhawk, and it has fussier habitat requirements and is subject to

DO IT YOURSELF

The area most renowned for its displaying goshawks is New Fancy View in the RSPB's Nagshead reserve (GL15 4LA), in the Forest of Dean. Peak skydancing season is March. ⌁ www.rspb.org/nagshead ☎ 01594 562852

You'll need to brush up on your bird ID skills. Like sparrowhawks, goshawks have broad wings and a broad tail, but they are larger with longer necks. There's a good guide to telling your British raptors (including goshawks) apart on the BBC: ⌁ www.bbc.co.uk/blogs/natureuk/entries/dcd6c3da-9952-40c2-884f-15cfdbabc9bd

Yorkshire Coast Nature runs days out in the Great Yorkshire Forest in the North York Moors National Park to watch and photograph goshawks. ⌁ yorkshirecoastnature.com/events/category/16/2018-wildlife-birdwatching ☎ 01723 865498

occasional persecution by gamekeepers. There are only an estimated 280-430 pairs in the whole of the UK.

Second, the goshawk is indeed a spectacular bird, with females nearly the size of a buzzard (males – as with many birds of prey – are about a third smaller), but it's a far more agile hunter that takes everything from hares and squirrels to crows, pigeons and even pheasants – it is for this last reason that they are regarded as pests by some gamekeepers and occasionally illegally persecuted. They are barrel-chested with fierce yellow-orange eyes, though I've never seen a goshawk either close enough or for long enough to appreciate them.

Unless you're an expert or have good local knowledge, you cannot plan to see a goshawk. The only time this doesn't hold true is for a month or so in the spring, when males are looking for a mate. Like many raptors, goshawks indulge in what are termed 'skydancing' displays, which involve aerial gymnastics to demonstrate to a female they're worth mating with.

The goshawk's begins just above the canopy of its territorial wood. The only time I've seen it, the male ascended almost vertically 30 metres or more, then plunged dramatically down again, repeating this several times for a good two minutes. The bird, which was already some 300 or 400 metres away, then flew off and was soon little more than a speck on the horizon. If nothing else, it gave me a taste of something I wanted to see again.

77 SCAVENGING RAVENS

SUGARLOAF MOUNTAIN AND THE BLACK MOUNTAINS

Family friendly ★★★

Sugarloaf Mountain is a relatively easy climb, even for young children

Budget friendly ★★★★★

Nothing to pay

Amateur friendly ★★★★

Hard to mistake the raven's deep crocking call for anything else – visually, it looks like a crow but is the size of a buzzard

Best time of year

Oct-March

The most menacing bird call you'll hear in Britain does not belong to one of our super-charged raptors such as peregrine falcons, goshawks or white-tailed eagles –

DO IT YOURSELF

The shortest route up Sugarloaf Mountain is from the carpark (marked on the Ordnance Survey map) about 4km north-west of Abergavenny town centre. From there, it's less than 3km to the summit.

There are ravens (and some red kites) throughout the Black Mountains, which are part of the Brecon Beacons NP. ⌖ www.breconbeacons.org/black-mountains. This website also has ideas for walking routes, and you can download routes to your mobile through websites such as go4awalk.com

There's a raven roost on Anglesey, in North Wales – some 800 ravens are said to roost in Newborough Forest during the winter. Don't go to Newborough Forest itself, however – instead, park at Pont Marquis, about 3km north-east of Malltraeth, at dusk and walk the marked footpath along Afon Cefni towards Malltraeth Marsh and Cors Ddyga RSPB Reserve.

these birds are largely silent, preferring perhaps to let their beaks and claws do the talking. No, it's the throaty, deep 'cronk' of a raven, and it rises up on the wind as if it has come from the mouth of the Grim Reaper. You frequently hear a raven before you see one, and it's always thrilling.

The walk to the top of Sugarloaf Mountain, just outside Abergavenny, provides good sightings, but one of my most memorable experiences with ravens – and one which sums up the nature of the bird – took place north of the tiny village of Llanbedr, a few miles outside of Crickhowell in the heart of the Black Mountains, while mountain biking.

First one, then two, then more, throaty cronks alerted me to their presence, and looking up I could see they were riding the winds on the hillside, watching me carefully. There were at least a dozen of them, and they weren't going away. I soon found out why – a sheep had collapsed and was lying prone on its side, still breathing, a bloody patch around one of its eyes.

I briefly considered putting it out of its misery, because this was clearly why the ravens were here in such force, but I didn't have the stomach for battering it to death. So, I left it to the tender mercies of those the ravens, hoping the end would come quickly. As I cycled on, a pair swept by, tumbling like acrobats in the steady wind, rushing onwards to the bounty that had suddenly presented itself. I couldn't help but admire their opportunism and zest.

76 LEKKING BLACK GROUSE

LANGDON BECK

Family friendly ★
No – you have to be up before the crack of dawn at one of the coldest times of year!

Budget friendly ★★★
The RSPB makes a small charge for its dates with nature, but a full-on tour will be much more expensive

Amateur friendly ★★★
Black grouse are easy to identify, though surprisingly hard to spot from a distance

Best time of year
Feb / March-April

Black grouse are extraordinary, jet-black birds a little bigger and a whole lot plumper than chickens. Relatives of red grouse (birds of heather moorland best known for being bred in their thousands to be shot), black grouse are woodland-edge birds, and in Britain are now restricted to Scotland, North and Mid-Wales and a few areas in northern England.

They are also renowned for a mating system called lekking, in which males face-off against each other as both a way of intimidating their rivals and to

DO IT YOURSELF

The RSPB runs guided black grouse days from March-May. Search online for RSPB Coed Llandegla
☎ 02920 353 008

Northern Experience Wildlife Tours run trips to see Black Grouse in Upper Teesdale.
🖱 www.northernexperiencewildlifetours.co.uk ☎ 01670 827465

The Glen Tanar estate (AB34 5EU), on the eastern edge of the Cairngorms, rents out hides to photograph black grouse – you get much closer to the birds than you would on an RSPB guided walk, but there's a catch: you have to be in the hide by 4.30am and stay until 8.30!
🖱 www.glentanar.co.uk/estate-activities/wildlife-photography ☎ 013398 86451

attract the females. Think of it as competitive dancing. They possess dramatic, pure-white tail feathers which are an important element in their armoury.

They are shy and easily disturbed, so it's hard to get close to them. I went on an RSPB black grouse 'Date with nature' at Coed Llandegla, Forestry Commission woodland west of Wrexham, in early April. We met at 5am and set off for the hide in darkness, arriving just as it was getting light. We were some 400 metres from the lekking arena, so even through binoculars it wasn't easy to see what was going on – a more powerful spotting scope would have been handy here.

Nevertheless, it was exciting to see the birds fly in like feathered bowling balls, all plumped up male bravado, white tail feathers on display like the latest iPhone on the bar-room table. What lekking took place was disappointingly brief, however, and many of the birds disappeared behind vegetation, and I can't say I'd recommend this to anyone with only a casual interest in wildlife.

Langdon Beck, in Upper Teesdale, is often cited as the best place to see black grouse in England. You can see them very easily from your car around the area of the Langdon Beck Hotel, or you could head west along the road that leads to the Cow Green Reservoir. Again, a very early start is essential – head out before first light and get breakfast at the hotel when you're done.

75 AVOCET CRUISE

RIVER EXE

Family friendly ★★
Not one for children unless they are very keen on birds

Budget friendly ★★★
Less than £20 for a 90 minute cruise

Amateur friendly ★★★★
RSPB guides come on the cruise, and in any case, avocets are easy to spot and identify

Best time of year
Dec-Feb

Think carefully – without looking, can you picture the RSPB's logo? It's mostly blue, and it's got the RSPB letters, but what's that black and white bird with the long bill? Well, yes, it's an avocet.

Avocets are the most elegant of waders with smart, unfussy monochrome plumage and a fabulously strange, upturned bill. During the winter, they retreat to the warmer climes of estuaries in southern Britain, and one of their big strongholds is the River Exe, which flows out to sea via Topsham and Dawlish Warren.

The cruises depart from Topsham, where the river is narrow and disintegrating wooden boat hulls litter the mudflats, and always at low

DO IT YOURSELF

Cruises run by the RSPB leave from Topsham between November and February. Numbers peak during the coldest months, usually January and February. Check the RSPB Bowling Green Marsh website for information about the cruises. 🖱 www.rspb.org/bowlinggreenmarsh ☎ 01392 833311

In Poole Harbour, a good place to see them is Brownsea Island, which is owned by the National Trust. Ferries are run by Brownsea Island Ferries. 🖱 www.brownseaislandferries.com ☎ 01929 462383

tide, because that's when the thousands of birds that overwinter here are feeding and easiest to see. Here you will see black-headed gulls loafing about on bright pink buoys and busy little redshanks – small brown waders with orange legs – probing around in the mud.

The Exe quickly widens into a vast expanse of mudflats that is a dinner table for some 20,000 birds during the coldest periods of the winter, including 600-700 avocets. On my trip, in mid-November (still too early in the winter to have peak numbers), we started seeing avocets straight away, at first in ones and twos. Then a flock of 30 or more, alarmed by the passing boat, took flight and wheeled around in a great piebald arc, over the narrow channel that is left at low tide and onto the flats on the other side.

Other, smaller groups were feeding in numbers of ten or fifteen down by the water's edge, their plumage reminiscent of the straight lines and bold contrasts of a piece of modern art, scything their upturned bills through the water in search of marine invertebrates.

Avocets neatly encapsulate the positive side of what's happened to our wildlife in the past half decade or more – while many species have declined, alarmingly in some cases, others have reappeared in Britain after being absent for many years. Avocets came back at the end of the Second World War in Suffolk and have since spread west. Catch them if you can.

74 BREEDING LAPWINGS

WESTRAY

Family friendly ★★

I can't say I've ever managed to interest my children in lapwings, but you won't have to walk far to see them

Budget friendly ★★★

Yes – apart from the cost of getting to Westray

Amateur friendly ★★★★

Lapwings are small, delicate-looking waders with very obvious crests on their heads

Best time of year

April-Sept

Sometimes referred to as the 'butterfly bird', because of their funny, flappy flying style and their rounded wings – the whole effect indeed mimicking a butterfly – lapwings

DO IT YOURSELF

You may find lapwings and curlews almost anywhere in the Orkney Islands, so keep an eye out wherever you are. The B9067 heading south from Pierowall on Westray would be a good place to start.

Ferries from the Orkney Mainland to Westray leave from Kirkwall. ✆ www.orkneyferries.co.uk/island_destinations.php?id=westray ☎ 01856 872044

Brodgar RSPB Reserve (KW16 3JZ), on the Orkney Mainland, would also be worth a visit and has breeding lapwings, curlews and oystercatchers. Plus, it's right next to the world-famous Ring of Brodgar, the 4,000-year-old (or so) stone circle. ✆ www.rspb.org/brodgar ☎ 01856 850176

Alternatively, try Cottascarth and Rendall Moss RSPB Reserve (KW17 2PA), which also has breeding curlews, cuckoos, hen harriers and short-eared owls. ✆ www.rspb.org/cottascarth ☎ 01856 850176

are wading birds that used to be common right across Britain. Numbers have been particularly badly hit in their breeding grounds in southern Britain, and outside of dedicated wildlife reserves, it's hard to find them in England at all, which is why I've recommended such a remote outpost of the British Isles to see a bird that could once have been found on almost any farm throughout the country.

When I visited Westray with my family, we stayed in a small self-catering cottage at Langskaill, near Berst Ness on the west side of the island. Driving from there to the main town, Pierowall, along the ramrod straight B9067, there were several cattle pastures where lapwings, curlews and the odd oystercatcher could be seen feeding during the day.

But there was one field that was as crammed with hungry diners as a five-star restaurant in a one horse town. Rows and rows of these smart little green, black and white waders lined up in the field, some searching for invertebrates in the soil while others merely stood in reflective silence, buffeted by some of the strongest winds I've ever experienced in my life. There must have been several hundred of them in a field not much larger than a football pitch, along with 20 or 30 curlews, larger waders with brown plumage and beautiful downward-curving bills.

If you're lucky, you may see the lapwing chicks, tiny balls of fluff that look from a distance as if they've got a golf ball growing out of the back of their heads, and possibly some of the most endearing baby birds you are ever likely to see.

73 ROCKPOOLING

SOUTH LANDING, FLAMBOROUGH

Family friendly ★★★★★
A brilliant activity for children

Budget friendly ★★★★★
You just need buckets or trays

Amateur friendly ★★★
You can have loads of fun
without any expertise, but
some knowledge or a seashore
species ID guide would come
in handy

Best time of year
All year round – but spring
and summer are probably best

Toilets ✓
Cafe ✓

If you include its thousands of islands, the UK has more than 30,000km of coastline, and while most of that isn't suitable for rockpooling, there have got to be tens, if not hundreds, of km in all areas of the country that is – so you might consider it daft to recommend a single location.

But, I'm going to, though South Landing, on Flamborough Head in north-east Yorkshire, is isn't a place for rockpooling as such, but more turning over rocks and stones at low tide to see what you find – and what finds you make. In less than an hour, a group of us found everything from green shore crabs and tiny pie-crust, brown crabs the size of vol-au-vents (with luck, these will grow into much larger edible ones) to fish such as rockling, butterfish – this one, resembling a tiny, slippery dragon – and even a baby plaice.

There were plenty of vivid-red beaded anemones, which retract their tentacles at low tide and look like strawberry lozenges one could happily chew, and chitons – sometimes called coat-of-mail shells for their armour-like plating – firmly attached to the undersides of the rocks and almost fossil-like in appearance. The strangest find was a 40cm-long paddleworm, a sea creature I'd never heard of before that leaves a sticky mucus staining your hands yellow if you pick it up.

You don't even need nets for this, just a bucket or (better still) some large, flat plastic trays so that you can see and photograph your finds more easily.

DO IT YOURSELF

South Landing is south of the village of Flamborough on South Sea Road. There's a car park at the Living Seas Centre (YO15 1AE), and the beach is another 100m down the road.

The Living Seas Centre has displays and can offer hot drinks and snacks – it's free to enter but there is a small charge for the car park. Yorkshire Wildlife Trust offers educational programmes for primary school children and occasional sea safaris (when the weather permits) between April and July.
🖱 www.ywt.org.uk/Living-Seas-Centre   ☎ 01262 422103

Devon Wildlife Trust runs rockpool safaris from its marine centre (PL9 0HP) in Wembury Bay (south-east of Plymouth) which are suitable for children aged 4 and over.
🖱 www.wemburymarinecentre.org   ☎ 01752 862538

The Wildlife Trusts has a selection of 24 of the best rockpooling beaches in the country on its website:
🖱 www.wildlifetrusts.org/where_to_see_rockpool_wildlife

There are dozens of rockpooling guidebooks available. *The Rockpool Guide: A Guide to some of the Plants and Animals to be Found on the Seashores of Britain*, by John Walters, is a laminated leaflet, so great for taking out and about.

72 SWAN LAKE

WELNEY WETLAND CENTRE

Family friendly ★★★★★
Easy viewing of whooper and Bewick's swans and other wildfowl in a comfortable hide

Budget friendly ★★★
Entrance to the WWT reserve costs just over £20 for a family of four (assuming children aged 4-16), but it's free to members

Amateur friendly ★★★★
Yes, but learn to tell your mute, Bewick's and whooper swans apart

Best time of year
Dec-Feb

Toilets ✓
Cafe ✓

© James Fair.

Everyone knows what a swan is, and they're really common, hardly something to put in a top 100 of Britain's wildlife experiences. Well, right – and wrong. Because there are swans and there are *wild* swans. The ones most people think of are mute swans, instantly recognisable with their dark-orange bills, and they can be seen in rivers and lakes here all-year-round.

But two other species visit our shores during the winter, fleeing the frigid Arctic tundra where they breed – whooper and Bewick's swans, and some 11,000 descend on the Ouse Washes that span Cambridgeshire and Norfolk between November and March. They're distinct from mute swans in having large patches of yellow on black bills (with the whoopers having more yellow than Bewick's), and they're smaller, more refined versions of their mute cousins.

The swans spend the day feeding on what's left of the sugar beet or potato harvest in nearby fields, but every evening they return to the washes to spend the night. Welney's hide overlooks a large semi-permanent lake, and every day (during the winter), the swans, plus assorted mallards and other ducks, get a 3.30pm and 6.30pm feed (the later one is Thursday-Sunday only), which brings them right underneath the hide.

When I visited in early December, it was still a bit early for the full swan spectacular, but it was still pretty good. As darkness descended, floodlights illuminated the graceful, snow-white birds gliding over the inky black water – swan lake, indeed. A few small groups – mum and dad and this year's offspring – flew in, just silhouettes against the darkening sky, swelling the numbers on the water.

In the distance, several thousand golden plovers and lapwings suddenly lifted into the air, moving this way and that. Two or three marsh harriers were patrolling the lake, though it was unclear whether it was them or a deadlier predator such as a peregrine falcon that had caused them to flock in such spectacular style.

71 PREDATORY GREAT SKUAS

HOY RSPB RESERVE

Family friendly ★★
Children may not fall in love with the rakish charm of the great skua, and Hoy is pretty wild at the best of times

Budget friendly ★★★★
Nothing to pay – apart from getting to Hoy

Amateur friendly ★★★
Menacing, gull-sized birds that are relatively easy to recognise

Best time of year
May-August

Great skuas, as someone once suggested to me, are gulls slowly evolving into eagles. With their mottled dark-brown plumage and white wing flashes (these only show in flight), it would be hard to confuse them with even great black-backed gulls, though they hold themselves in a very similar way and have webbed feet. But they're larger and meaner with a huge beak that suggests they mean business. And they do.

DO IT YOURSELF

To access Hoy RSPB Reserve, the RSPB recommends either parking at Rackwick or the Dwarfie Stane, a 5,000-year-old monument of hollowed-out sandstone.
🖱 www.rspb.org/hoy   ☎ 01856 850176

Other great locations for great skuas in Orkney include North Hill on the island of Papa Westray and Noup Cliffs on Westray.

Hermaness National Nature Reserve (NNR), on the Shetland island of Unst, also has bonxies.
🖱 www.nature.scot/enjoying-outdoors/places-visit/scotlands-national-nature-reserves/hermaness-nnr/hermaness-nnr-visiting-reserve

Gulls are mainly scavengers but great skuas – referred to by their Shetland name of 'bonxie' throughout Scotland – are truly predatory. Like hyenas taking kills from less powerful hunters, they'll happily steal a catch from other seabirds, either out at sea or as they're bringing home a precious meal for their chicks – behaviour known as kleptoparasitism. I've read that they can attack and steal catches from birds as big as gannets, and they'll also attack and eat puffins, which they can pretty much down in one piratical gulp.

In Britain, you'll find them in north-west Scotland and Scottish islands, but perhaps the best place to go is the RSPB's reserve on Hoy, the most westerly of the Orkney Islands, where some 1,900 pairs breed – an estimated 12 per cent of the entire world population.

There's some excellent walking all over Hoy, but for bonxies, take the coastal trail from Rackwick or the tiny hamlet of Moorfea. It starts off following the cliff tops, then cuts inland across moorland where you should see the great skuas. If you stray too close to a nest, they may dive-bomb you, and the advice is to hold a hand or stick above your head and move away.

This trail takes you to the Old Man of Hoy itself, well worth seeing especially if there are any climbers scaling this iconic sandstone crag. If you're feeling brave, you could return to the ferry port at Moaness via Moor Fea and the well-marked trail in the Glens of Kinnaird and Sandy Loch (another good place to see bonxies). You'll need the Ordnance Survey map, but it's not a long walk and easy to navigate.

70 CHOUGHS

BARDSEY ISLAND

Family friendly ★
Bardsey not ideal for young children – there's little to do apart from watch wildlife or walk round the island

Budget friendly ★★
You can take occasional day trips to Bardsey, otherwise you have to stay there

Amateur friendly ★★★
With their red bills and legs, choughs are very distinctive

Best time of year
Spring, summer or early autumn

Toilets ✓
Self-catering kitchen and store ✓

It may not sound remarkable, but it still makes me smile that the Bird Observatory on Bardsey Island is the only place I've ever stayed where I've been able to hear both chickens and choughs at the same time.

DO IT YOURSELF

Bardsey is less than 2km off the tip of the Lleyn Peninsula in North Wales. It is owned by the Bardsey Island Trust, and it has nine cottages, ranging from a five-bedroomed farmhouse to a single bedroom cottage, for rent between April and October. None of the houses has electricity, and no cars are allowed on the island. ✆ www.bardsey.org ☎ 08458 112233

You can also stay at Bardsey Lodge and Bird Observatory, which is basic but perfectly comfortable and has cooking facilities. ✆ www.bbfo.org.uk ☎ 01626 773908

Boats to Bardsey are run from Porth Meudwy by Mordaith Llŷn, and generally they only happen on Saturdays. ✆ www.bardseyboattrips.com ☎ 07971 769895

You can also see choughs in Pembrokeshire and Cornwall. ✆ www.cornishchoughs.org ☎ 01392 453775

Choughs are members of the crow family, so related to some of the commonest birds found in Britain today – carrion crows, jackdaws, magpies and rooks – but in contrast, they're only found in coastal areas and are really very rare: no more than 350 pairs in the whole of Britain, all of them found on the west coast from Cornwall as far north as southern Scotland. So, choughs are mainly found in places far from human habitation, not where people are raising domestic chickens.

The other thing about choughs is, though like most other crows, they're plumage is pretty much jet black, they differ in having orange-red feet and bills. They have a lovely soft call, as well, not unlike a jackdaw's, and they're skilful fliers renowned for their tumbling flight displays and they seem to enjoy playing around in stiff sea breezes for the sheer pleasure of it.

During the breeding season, you'll see them in pairs, with each one claiming its own territory along a stretch of coastline. In the autumn and winter, they form larger groups that can be really quite spectacular.

I visited Bardsey in mid-September, so it was also a great time of year because the grey seals were in full pupping season. It's a wild, beautiful island at the end of the Lleyn Peninsula, and you can walk round most of the island in two or three hours. With ten or so chough breeding territories on the island (which should amount to ten pairs), the chances are you'll run into some sooner or later.

69 WHISTLING SIKA DEER

ARNE RSPB RESERVE, NEAR WAREHAM

Family friendly ★★★
Relatively easy to find the deer, especially if they're whistling

Budget friendly ★★★★
If you're not RSPB members, there's a small car parking charge

Amateur friendly ★★★★
Easy enough to identify – a touch smaller than red deer, they are dark grey or red in the winter, spotty in the summer

Best time of year
Sept-Oct

Toilets ✓

For deer that are just a little smaller than our native red deer, sikas make the most unlikely vocalisation, often referred to as a whistle, though I'd describe it as sounding more like a door that is opening very slowly on rusty hinges. Sika stags do this during the rutting season, which runs from late September to mid-October,

DO IT YOURSELF

Arne RSPB Reserve (BH20 5BJ) is in the Isle of Purbeck in Dorset. It's a heathland (so heather blooms here in the late summer) and oak woodland habitat and apart from its sika deer and birds, particularly noted for its dragonflies and reptiles. ☝ www.rspb.org/arne ☎ 01929 553360

It's worth asking at the small visitor centre where you're most likely to find any deer, as they move about.

Sika deer can also be found in the New Forest in Hampshire (an estimated 100 or so near Brockenhurst), though the greatest numbers are in north-west Scotland. Some in Cumbria and Lancashire, too.

and Arne is a great place to go because the chances are there'll be a stag in one of the fields a short walk below the car park, and he'll be trying to attract and keep a harem – the whistling noise is his way of telling other males to back off.

On my only visit to Arne during the rutting season, we saw a large stag and some hinds in an open field, but all was quiet. We wandered down to the beach, which gives you a view onto Poole Harbour, and it was only on the way back that I was halted in my tracks by a sound that felt all wrong in a wild place. For a moment, I was confused, and then I remembered – a sika stag, of course! We were walking through a small patch of woodland, and just managed to catch him as he slunk away into the trees.

Sika deer originally came from Japan, China, Taiwan and the Russian Far East (though today, they're mainly confined to Japan) and can interbreed with red deer to which they are closely related, producing impure hybrids.

They first came to Dorset when they were introduced onto Brownsea Island, in Poole Harbour (Arne is a mini peninsula poking out into the harbour from its southern side), and they escaped to the mainland by swimming. And though they are now an accepted part of the wildlife of this part of southern England, the fact is they also need to be culled on a regular basis to stop them having a negative impact on other fauna and flora.

68 DAFFODIL TRAIL

FARNDALE

Family friendly ***
Even for children who don't appreciate flowers, there are fields and woods to rampage through

Budget friendly *****
Unless you go overboard on the cream teas afterwards

Amateur friendly *****
Everyone knows a daffodil when they see one

Best time of year
March (but up to early May in Scotland)

© James Fair

Most people don't need a book, or indeed assistance of any kind, to find a daffodil in this country. These days, some varieties start flowering as early as December, and they continue to bloom into early May in the north of Scotland, and they're everywhere.

DO IT YOURSELF

The Farndale Trail starts at Low Mill, on the southern side of North York Moors National Park, and it's a linear route of about 5.5km. ⌂ www.northyorkmoors.org.uk/visiting/enjoy-outdoors/walking/our-walks/walking-routes/farndale ☎ 01439 772700

Gloucestershire's Golden Triangle is near Newent, to the west of Gloucester. I started at Gwen and Vera's Fields Nature Reserve (after parking in the carpark at Shaw Common), walked north on footpaths to Betty Daw's Wood, then returned along the quiet road via Park Wood. Gloucestershire Wildlife Trust: ⌂ www.gloucestershirewildlifetrust.co.uk/nature-reserves/gwen-and-veras-fields ☎ 01452 383333

It's said Wordsworth wrote *Daffodils* after visiting Glencoyne Bay on Ullswater in the Lake District. Both there and Dora's Field, at Rydal Mount (his former home) are said to have fine daffodil displays still. ⌂ www.rydalmount.co.uk ☎ 015394 33002

But most, or many, of the daffodils you see are domesticated ones, pale hybrid imitations of their wild ancestors, some with those faintly ridiculous, orange trumpets or paler outer petals. There's something about real wild daffodils that hits you when you see them – they're smaller and less showy than domesticated ones, but close-up the colours are sharper, just that little bit more yellow, as if the flowers have been distilled down to a purer, more concentrated form of their daffodil essence.

The Farndale Trail, which follows the course of the River Dove in the North York Moors National Park, is the most famous daffodil trail in Britain, but I don't have first-hand knowledge of it. A few years ago, I did I walk Gloucestershire's aptly named Golden Triangle with my then four-year-old son. Clumps of bright yellow daffodils greeted us around almost every twist in the trail, and enterprising local residents open up their houses with offers of tea and cakes.

Best of all is the delightful Gwen and Vera's Fields Nature Reserve – a field so full of wild daffs, it's more yellow than green. The best time to go is mid-March, which is also a good time of year to listen out for the spring's first chiffchaffs tootling their cheerful two-note song among the leafless branches, an indication – like the sun-filled daffodil blooms – that everything is about to burst into life.

Daffodils may not have the rapacious thrill of a deadly white-tailed eagle, but there is something to be said for a pleasant walk in flower-filled woodlands followed by a saturated-fat-filled wedge of Victoria sponge.

67 SINGING SKYLARKS

PEWSEY DOWNS NNR

Family friendly ★★★
I've never found children appreciate the remarkable skylark, but it's a beautiful place for a walk

Budget friendly ★★★★★
At least it's free!

Amateur friendly ★★★★
Learning to recognise the skylark's song isn't hard

Best time of year
Late March-June

If there were a prize for the feistiest bird in Britain, then it would surely go to the skylark, especially if you combined some co-efficient of gutsiness with a factorial relating to size. In short, they are small birds with a lot to shout about.

DO IT YOURSELF

Pewsey Downs National Nature Reserve is a classic skylark location, with wildflowers and butterflies and a white horse dating back to 1812. There's a carpark about 1-1.5km north of the village of Alton Priors, and from there it's a short walk to the reserve. ⌨ www.gov.uk/government/publications/pewsey-downs-nnr-public-access-for-horse-riding-and-cycling ☎ 07771 944557

Much of the farmland within the Marlborough Downs and nearby Salisbury Plain is good for skylarks.

Exmoor is also an excellent location for skylarks – they could be anywhere, but try its highest point, Dunkery Beacon, 2km to the north-west of Wheddon Cross, and within the National Trust's Holnicote Estate. ⌨ www.nationaltrust.org.uk/holnicote-estate ☎ 01643 862452

A slightly different skylark site is Saltholme RSPB Reserve (TS2 1TP) at the mouth of the River Tees. ⌨ www.rspb.org/saltholme ☎ 01642 546625

Skylarks are birds of open arable fields in both lowland and upland areas, and as a result, they don't – like most normal birds – nest somewhere safe like a nice high tree or inaccessible cavity in a riverbank, but on the ground. It leaves their chicks vulnerable to predation, and makes the adults feel, well, just a touch paranoid.

Walking through a field, common or across moorland where skylarks nest, you inevitably pass close to their nests, and when that happens, up pops a male, ascending perhaps 30 metres vertically into the air, to tell you in no uncertain terms if you wouldn't mind moving on. It's a long, drawn-out communication, not (in my view, though the poet Percy Shelley, who wrote the famous To a Skylark, would disagree) the most beautiful birdsong in Britain, but certainly a thing of wonder and mystery.

Male skylarks are also trying to attract a mate, of course, and their song is an essential part of their armoury – look at me, it's saying, I can fly higher and sing louder than any of the other boys around here. Skylarks are also the first birds to start singing in the morning, well before first light – we don't say 'Up with the lark' for nothing.

Apart from the song, the most obvious distinguishing feature of skylarks is the small crests on the top of their heads, which are raised when they are excited or alarmed. Otherwise, they are small (about the size of a starling) and streaky-brown – but you'll know one when you hear one.

66 GREATER HORSESHOE BATS

BUCKFASTLEIGH

Family friendly ★★★
One of Britain's largest bats, with a wingspan of up to 40cm

Budget friendly ★★★★
A small charge to pay for a guided walk

Amateur friendly ★★
You may need an expert to find and identify the bats

Best time of year
June-July

© Mike Symes.

I've never been to see the greater horseshoe bats at Buckfastleigh, but I'm pretty sure this would make a tremendous spectacle, because I have been lucky enough to see a few of them – in my own back garden.

DO IT YOURSELF

The Devon Greater Horseshoe Bat Project has more information about its bats and will organise guided walks on request. ⌗ devonbatproject.org ☎ 01392 279244

Woodchester Mansion is an unfinished gothic stately home in the grounds of Woodchester Park, and a maternity roost for both greater and lesser horseshoes. For bat walks: ⌗ www.woodchestermansion.org.uk/Bats.aspx ☎ 01453 861541

Woodchester Park (GL10 3TS) is owned by the National Trust. Confusingly, the entrance to the park is just outside the village of Nympsfield, not Woodchester as you'd expect. ⌗ www.nationaltrust.org.uk/woodchester-park ☎ 01452 814213

Greater horseshoes are one of our rarest species of bat, and only found today in the South-west of England and South Wales. I do, however, live near a relatively large colony at Woodchester Mansion, in Gloucestershire. I've been bat detecting up there with the local bat group (we didn't see any but did hear some lesser horseshoes on the detectors), and during the summer, you can watch them roosting in the roof on CCTV.

That's where I learned that greater and lesser horseshoes are the only bats we have in this country that can hang upside down by clinging on with their claws. They also wrap their wings around their bodies, presumably to keep the heat in.

A few years after the trip to Woodchester Park, I was in the garden one evening in July just as it was getting dark when I noticed there were a few bats, perhaps three or four, flying around in the warm summer air. But they weren't just any bats – they were huge. Our most common species in this country are pipistrelles, and they're tiny little creatures with bodies half the size that of a mouse.

These bats were so big they reminded me of fruit bats, enormous creatures found in tropical countries and nothing like our insect-eating bats. For a moment, I couldn't work it out, but then I remembered the greater horseshoe colony up the road in Woodchester Park.

But while I saw just a few that evening, the caves in Buckfastleigh are home to an estimated 1,500 in the summer, which in itself is about 25 per cent of the known population in Britain. The Bat Conservation Trust says they have a body the size of a small pear and a wingspan of 35-40cm (though other sources suggest they're a little smaller than that). It adds that they appear bigger than other bats because they usually fly closer to the ground, just 2 metres or lower in general.

65 BASKING ADDERS

HUMBERHEAD PEATLANDS NNR

Family friendly ★★★★
Despite its reputation, the adder is not dangerous to humans

Budget friendly ★★★★
There will be a small charge for the guided walk

Amateur friendly ★
Adders can be surprisingly hard to spot

Best time of year
Feb-April

I don't think the list of Britain's 100 top wildlife experiences would be complete without a snake in it, though I know they are not everybody's favourite animals. We only have three native species in Britain – the grass snake, which can turn up just about anywhere, but particularly loves watery landscapes; the smooth snake, which is rare and

DO IT YOURSELF

Humberhead Peatlands National Nature Reserve, sandwiched between Doncaster and Scunthorpe in South Yorkshire, has a reputation for being one of the best places in Britain to see adders. Guided walks take place in February and March. ⌨ www.humberheadpeatlands.org.uk ☎ 01302 846014

To see adders in the Wyre Forest, leave the town of Bewdley on Dry Mill Lane, then take the track on your left before you reach the bottom of the hill. Go along this track until you reach an area of bracken, some trees and shrubs. Look for adders basking at the base of trees, and also common lizards on dead tree trunks or rocks.

Adders like heathland, open woodland and mire habitats. South-west Scotland and South Wales are also strongholds. The Amphibian and Reptile Conservation Trust has excellent information about adders. ⌨ www.arc-trust.org/adder ☎ 01202 391319

only found in heathland habitats in southern England; and the adder, our only venomous snake.

And of these, the adder is the easiest to see – or, at least, the most predictable. In late February, the males emerge from hibernation, needing time to feed up before they are ready to mate. At this time of year, there's very little new vegetation, which makes it easier to spot them as they bask (on clear mornings) in the early spring sunshine.

That doesn't make it easy, however, as I found out when I went adder-hunting in the Wyre Forest in Worcestershire. Despite having a line of dark zig-zags running along their back, and a background colouration ranging from light grey to copper and brown, they are remarkably well camouflaged on a bed of dead, brown bracken. 'Look, there's two there, under that bush,' said my guide, the adder expert Sylvia Sheldon, but it took me an age to spot them, and I'd have marched straight past them without her help.

They're not big, either, growing to a maximum of 60cm in length, but there is still something exciting about seeing a venomous snake in the wild. While they are not aggressive and rarely bite, it is said to be acutely painful – just almost never fatal: there have been ten recorded deaths from adder bites in the past 100 years.

If you were really lucky, you might see the apparently spectacular adder dance, when two males stand up and twist round each other as they seek to lay claim to a territory.

64 OWL PROWL

WOODLAND AND GRASSLAND

Family friendly ★★★
It's a night-time activity, but in the winter and early spring, that doesn't mean you have to go out late

Budget friendly ★★★★
Worth having a good torch

Amateur friendly ★★★
Yes – but learn the tawny owl's hoots and calls before you go

Best time of year
Late autumn and early winter, and (it's said) two hours after sunset

A light drizzle had just set in as I left my house. I wasn't going far – there's a small area of woodland surrounding an open pasture in a valley just ten minutes' walk away. I'd been there many times, both night and day, but never specifically in search of tawny owls. I was hoping to see one, as well as hear it – so, I took a powerful torch, just in case.

DO IT YOURSELF

Where you go is the most important thing. Look at an Ordnance Survey map of your neighbourhood and try to identify woodland, possibly adjoining an open area, with a footpath or bridlepath for access. Parkland areas would be a good bet, and anywhere else there are plenty of trees, such as churchyards. Try listening out from your house and see if you can hear any.

Learn to identify owl calls – males usually make the familiar hooting call ('Whoo-hoo' or just 'Whoo'), while the female's is traditionally written as 'Kewick' – it's higher pitched than the male's. The two together make the 'Toowit (Kewick)-twoo (Whoo)' call that many people associate with tawny owls.

Wild Owl TV has recordings of both these calls (and those of other native British owls).
🖰 wildowl.co.uk/owlcalls.html

As I entered the pasture, which is enveloped on three sides by steeply sloping woodland, I was struck by how silent everything was. Nearing the end of the valley, it was still ominously quiet, but then I saw something reflected in the torchlight – a pair of eyes staring back at me, and which then moved back into the safety of the woodland.

I was fairly confident they belonged to a deer, almost certainly a roe deer. Three more pairs of eyes materialised on the other side of the valley and likewise disappeared, then a lone individual, this one close enough for me to see its white rump – definitely a roe.

Finally I heard some calls – first, the soft 'Kewicks' of a female tawny owl off to the left. I started to walk up through the precipitous beech wood to see if I could home in on the caller, but either it heard me coming or it was further away than I'd assumed. Then a male 'Whoo-hoo' boomed out down in the valley, so I retraced my steps.

It was probably purely by chance that I caught the owl in my torchlight, looking surprisingly large and cumbersome and with a paler chest than I'd expected. There's a tumbledown farm building in the valley, and I can only assume it had been using it as a perch. It wasn't hanging around, and like the deer, it had soon disappeared into the night.

63 BAT DETECTING

WOODLANDS, LAKES & RIVERS

Family friendly ★★★★★
Children love listening in to
bat-chat

Budget friendly ★★
A sufficiently good bat detector
will set you back by about £100
or more

Amateur friendly ★★★
While some expertise is useful,
you can learn as you go along

Best time of year
May-October

© James Fair.

Bat detecting is a bit like picking up communication signals from aliens. I don't mean there is anything other-worldly about bats, but simply picking up and translating their high frequency calls (which we can't hear with the 'naked' ear), usually a steady stream of tuts

---

DO IT YOURSELF

The Bat Conservation Trust has encyclopaedic information about bats on its website, including how to make contact with your local bat group. ☝ www.bats.org.uk/support-bats/bat-groups ☎ 0345 1300 228

☎ Alternatively, call 01786 822107 for Scottish Bat Groups and 01269 268768 for Welsh Bat Groups.

There are a huge variety of bat detectors available. Think about going on a guided bat walk before buying one to see what works for you and/or your children. I've found the Magenta Bat5 easy to use (☝ www.magenta2000.co.uk/acatalog/Bat_Detector_Bat5.html) and one of the cheapest. Alternatively, try a specialist retailer such as NHBS to see what other bat detectors are available. ☝ www.nhbs.com ☎ 01803 865913

Different bat species echolocate at different frequencies, and you'll need to find these out, but most bat detector manufacturers will provide this information with the kit.

and chirrups, is like decoding messages from another life form – though the bats, of course, are making them to be able to locate and eat airborne insects.

Anyone can bat detect, and apart from knowing where to go, you don't need to be an expert. There are dozens of local bat groups around the country that will do guided bat walks, and these are good places to start. It's also something that that young children, even as young as four or five, enjoy, and I think there are a number of reasons for this. First, there are gadgets with knobs to twiddle and buttons to press; second, they get to wear a head torch; and third, there are the bats, even if you may only hear (as opposed to see) them.

Bats can be found throughout Britain and are strictly protected, but as a general rule head for woodland areas or anywhere with freshwater, particularly still ponds and lakes, though slow-moving rivers can be good too. We have 17 species in this country, but the ones you are most likely to hear (and hopefully see too) are pipistrelles, which could be flitting about your garden even in quite suburban places.

Daubenton's bats are another good one to look and listen out for – they fly low over ponds and lakes – while noctules fly high in the sky over fields in lazy arcs. But, in my view, don't worry too much about what's what – just get out there and start listening. Who knows what you will find?

62 GREAT BUSTARDS

SALISBURY PLAIN

Family friendly ★
I can't see children getting especially excited by this

Budget friendly ★★★★
A small charge is made for the guided trip

Amateur friendly ★★★★★
No danger of mistaking the extraordinary great bustard for anything else

Best time of year
March-April

© James Farr.

The chances are you've never heard of the great bustard. You may briefly titter at its name (it actually comes, in a roundabout sort of way as these things often do, from the Latin for 'slow bird') and then wonder why a species that is sometimes described as the world's heaviest flying bird – I mean, that's quite a claim to fame, isn't it? – has passed you by for so long.

The truth is, some people don't regard it as a native British bird. That is to say, it was native, but became extinct here in the early part of the nineteenth century through overhunting and habitat loss, and for various reasons, a reintroduction initiative that has been going on in two small reserves on

---

DO IT YOURSELF

The Great Bustard Group runs guided trips throughout the year but recommends the lekking season as the best time to go. ⌘ greatbustard.org ☎ 07817 971327

The group likes to keep the locations of its two reserves quiet, so I was asked not to put it in print (you get picked up in a minibus and taken there), but as an indication, it's some 12km north of Stonehenge, just off the A345.

Salisbury Plain, in Wiltshire, since 2004 has never truly caught the public imagination.

All of which is a great shame, because this is a spectacular and oddly hypnotic bird. It can grow to a metre tall (the height of an average four-year-old) and can weigh more than 20kg – as the brains behind the reintroduction efforts, David Waters, pointed out to me, that's your maximum baggage allowance on most international flights.

They are beautiful too (if unusual in appearance) with stunning, snowy white feathers on their breasts, striking tortoiseshell backs and grey necks, and during the breeding season, males form amazing 'leks' (something black grouse also do, **Experience 76**) in which they compete with each other to earn the right to mate. You can watch these leks (from a distance) on a Great Bustard Group guided tour in March and April.

But there's something else about great bustards. Though not exclusively birds of arid grassland and steppe-type environments, that is certainly where they are generally found – more than half the world's population today is found in Spain. David took me to see a group of newly released birds that were still getting supplemental food, and as they ran towards us over the chalky soil of Salisbury Plain, their attitude and demeanour called to mind a much larger bird of the Africa savannah – the ostrich. Why we wouldn't want such charismatic and seemingly intelligent animals in our countryside, I can but wonder.

61 NESTING KINGFISHERS

RYE MEADS RSPB RESERVE, HERTFORDSHIRE

Family friendly ★★★
Dazzlingly beautiful birds, but will children keep quiet in a hide?

Budget friendly ★★★★
The RSPB asks non-members to pay £3 for parking

Amateur friendly ★★★★
Easy to recognise the kingfisher – and at Rye Meads the difficulty of spotting them is removed, too

Best time of year
April-June

Toilets ✓

I f you've ever had that feeling that kingfishers are deliberately avoiding you, you're not alone. You fetch up at a stretch of river that's supposed to be so chock-full of them it should be like finding pigeons in Trafalgar Square and you catch not even a sniff of that insanely

DO IT YOURSELF

Rye Meads RSPB Reserve (SG12 8JS, open from 9am) is close to the town of Hoddesdon – Rye House station (trains from Liverpool Street) is about a 5-10-minute walk away. ᗡ www.rspb.org/ryemeads ☎ 01992 708383

For an urban kingfisher experience, walk a stretch of the River Frome in Bristol on the footpath running from Broom Hill to Eastville, but any stretch could yield a sighting.

Tophill Low Nature Reserve (YO25 9RH), near Driffield in East Yorkshire, has a reputation as a good kingfisher spot. ᗡ tophilllow.blogspot.co.uk ☎ 01377 270690

Nature Photography Hides has a kingfisher hide near Droitwich, in Worcestershire, that it rents out for £99 a day. ᗡ www.naturephotographyhides.co.uk 07850 878370

iridescent blue back or zingy orange breast – the infuriating thing is they're probably there, you're just not seeing them.

They're tiny birds and they can spend a lot of time sitting very still on branches overhanging a river. Often all you see of one – if you see anything at all – is a flash of blue and orange as it takes flight, though this is always a thrill. Canoeing down the Wye some years ago, I spotted four or five kingfishers in the space of two or three hours as we disturbed them from their perches, and we tracked them as they streaked across the river like balls of burning blue.

More recently, I'd been told the River Frome in Bristol was an excellent place to see kingfishers, and just as I thought we'd miss out, there it was, perched on tree, not 15 metres away. We had about half a second to feast our eyes on its gorgeous beauty, and it was off.

But I've recommended Rye Meads, because it's got something most reserves haven't – artificial kingfisher nesting holes on a small lake very close to a hide. I've been to Rye Meads (but not during the breeding season), and it's very obvious this would be an amazing place to watch the birds as they fly to and from their nest feeding their chicks.

My only reservation is that some comments on the reserve's website suggested there are photographers who get to the hides early (especially at weekends) and don't make way for people who just want to get a quick glance of these fabulous birds. Weekdays are likely to be quieter or get there as early as you can.

60 REINDEER

GLENMORE, CAIRNGORMS NP

Family friendly ★★★★★
What child doesn't want to see Rudolph in the flesh? It's about a half hour walk to see them up the mountainside

Budget friendly ★★★
A family of four may pay up to £44, less if children are under 5

Amateur friendly ★★★★★
If you can't recognise Rudolph when you see him…

Best time of year
You can visit most of the year, though Christmas, surely?

Toilets ✓

It's hard not to warm to reindeer. Adapted as they are to living in frigid climates, they possess furry noses and hooves and shaggy coats that make them look like living, breathing soft toys, and they exhibit a permanent air of stoicism that I guess you need when the temperature's down to -15°C. And they pull Santa's sleigh.

They're record-breakers, too. They are the world's most northerly-living herbivore, and some in Alaska (where they're called caribou, though they are the same animal) undertake the longest migration of any land mammal – some 5,000km every year.

Thousands of years ago, they were living here in Britain, but they died out probably as a result of climate change and the reforestation of our landscape at

---

DO IT YOURSELF

The Cairngorm Reindeer herd is located in the northern part of the Cairngorms, close to Glenmore Visitor Centre and Loch Morlich. 🖱 www.cairngormreindeer.co.uk   ☎ 01479 861228

You can visit the herd all year round, except in January and the first half of February.

the end of the Ice Age. Then, in 1952, an anthropologist called Ethel Lindgren, together with her husband a Sami reindeer herder Mikel Utsi, brought over a small number of animals to show they would thrive in the Arctic conditions of the Cairngorms.

They did, and now the herd numbers 150. You can either take a hike up the mountain to see the reindeer living a semi-wild existence, and here you're welcome to hand-feed them and take photos. If you do want to go at Christmas, then be warned: the weather in the Cairngorms can get pretty wild at that time of year.

If you can't manage a hike into up the mountainside, then a smaller group of animals are kept in paddocks at the Reindeer Centre. This isn't all-year-round, however, and you can't handfeed these, but you can stroke them if they come up to you.

I confess I haven't been to the Reindeer Centre (I'd love to take my kids), but on a trip to Svalbard many years ago, we ran across a small herd on the bleak Arctic tundra. It was summer then, so the animals were in dark, chocolate-brown summer coats that turn – for obvious reasons – much paler in the winter. They crept along a precarious scree slope, seemingly oblivious to our presence. There are no obvious predators of reindeer on Svalbard, apart from possibly the occasional polar bear during the long summer months when they cannot hunt on the sea ice, but they were clearly wary.

The Cairngorm reindeer have no such anxieties, though there's always the worry they won't be asked to pull the sleigh.

59 STRANDED PORTUGUESE MAN O' WAR

PORTHERAS COVE

Family friendly ★★★

Yes – but don't let your kids touch them, and be wary about swimming where strandings have taken place

Budget friendly ★★★★★

Most beaches are free!

Amateur friendly ★★★★

Could be mistaken for jellyfish but the sail and tentacles are dead giveaways

Best time of year

Sept-Oct

I remember first reading about the extraordinary Portuguese man o' war in one of the children's wildlife adventure series books by Willard Price when I was a kid. I vaguely recall a scene in which either Hal or Roger, the two brothers who travel the world collecting animals for their father's zoo (yes, these books wouldn't get written today), got entangled in the man o' war's venomous tentacles.

Just the idea of this creature, that floats on water using an inflated sail to move and catches and immobilises prey with deadly arms up to 30 metres long, seemed both impossibly exotic and terrifying in equal measure.

So, to stumble across several on a beach in west Wales – stranded by a combination of strong south-westerlies and an ebbing tide – took me back

---

DO IT YOURSELF

Sightings of Portuguese men o' war are reported to Cornwall Wildlife Trust's Marine Strandings Network. Check the trust's website for further information. ⌖ www.cornwallwildlifetrust.org.uk/strandings ☎ 01872 273 939

The Marine Conservation Society may also have information on strandings. ⌖ www.mcsuk.org ☎ 01989 566017

to memories of reading and loving those books. I'd never have thought then that I'd ever see one here.

They are utterly bizarre animals – most of their bulk is that floating sail, which is bulbous at one end and forms a kind of frilly, pink-tinged sail on top. Underneath are the deadly tentacles coloured a purply-blue. The biology of these animals is even stranger than their appearance. For a start, they're not jellyfish as is generally assumed, but animals called siphonophores, and even more astonishingly, they're not a single animal, but four genetically identical ones that perform specialist tasks for the organism as a whole – floating, predating, feeding and reproduction

It's thought that men o' war are washing up on our beaches in the south and west of Britain for two reasons – first, warming sea temperatures as a result of climate change may be slowly pushing their range further north, and second, an increase in strong south-westerlies (probably a climate-change related issue as well), especially around September and October, are causing them to strand.

For that reason, I wouldn't mainly recommend the beach where we came across them – Marloes, in Pembrokeshire – because if they are going to turn up anywhere, it's more likely to be Cornwall and the Scilly Isles. Around the same time that we found a dozen or so at Marloes, volunteers in Cornwall were reporting more than 500 at Portheras Cove, between St Ives and Land's End on the north coast. The Marine Conservation Society (MCS) has reported in previous years large numbers at Newgale (also in Pembrokeshire) and Pendeen, Porth, Holywell Bay, Polzeath, Hayle and Tolcarne in Cornwall.

© James Fair.

58 SEA KAYAKING WITH SEALS

PEMBROKESHIRE

Family friendly ★
Not for young children

Budget friendly ★★
You can do guided day courses for about £100

Amateur friendly ★★★★
Seals aren't hard to spot or identify

Best time of year
August-Oct

On the west coast of Wales, female grey seals give birth to their pups from August until November, mostly seeking secluded beaches or sea caves in which to do so. Some of these pups – which start off life as pale as a polar bear and as fat as a witchetty grub – are easily visible from cliff-tops, but many lie hidden from view.

And with good reason, of course. For the first three weeks of their lives, the pups cannot swim and are completely defenceless. They lie there, developing

DO IT YOURSELF

There are are a number of adventure sports companies in Pembrokeshire that offer both sea kayaking courses and guided trips. I can recommend both TYF, which operates out of St Davids (🖰 www.tyf.com ☎ 01437 721611) and Sea Kayak Guides (🖰 seakayakguides. co.uk ☎ 07432 660235 or 07855 194533. My trip around Dinas Head was with Martin Leonard of Sea Kayak Guides.

But there are hundreds of great locations in Britain that are brilliant for sea kayaking. I've also done it in the Outer Hebrides (on Harris), and I'd certainly recommend it there, though I can't specifically vouch for this firm. Clearwater Paddling 🖰 www.clearwaterpaddling.com ☎ 01871 810 443

the layer of blubber they'll need before they lose their fluffy white coat and are ready to go to sea – and, on the whole, it's better to leave them well alone.

But in a sea kayak, you can watch the pups without disturbing them. In a kayak, you can be quiet and highly manoeuvrable, and using one allows you to observe the pups without doing any harm.

One of the best days I've had in a sea kayak was with Martin Leonard of Sea Kayak Guides. We set out from the small beach at Cwm yr Eglwys, in northern Pembrokeshire, and started to paddle around Dinas Head. The coastline here – like much of Pembrokeshire – is a fractal maze of indentations, and we were soon poking our kayaks into tiny bays and huge, dark sea caves. At the back of one, we could see the pale figure of a whitecoat staring back at us with huge eyes. We stayed at the entrance so as not to alarm either the pup or its mother, who we couldn't see in the half-light. We saw another and its mother in a more exposed spot further around the head.

On the way back, two peregrines streaked past us like laser-guided missiles, siblings, Martin said, that had hatched just a few months ago. With their healthy populations of rock doves (the real relative of the much-maligned urban pigeon), the sea cliffs of Pembrokeshire are rich hunting grounds for the world's fastest bird. More surprisingly, an otter surfaced just ten metres from our canoes, blinking at us in mild astonishment before quickly diving and disappearing into the grey-green swell.

57 BOOMING BITTERNS

HAM WALL RSPB RESERVE, NEAR ASHCOTT

Family friendly ★
Probably not exciting for children

Budget friendly ★★★★
There's a small carpark charge at Ham Wall

Amateur friendly ★★★
The bittern's boom is unique, but you may wonder what it is if you've never heard it before

Best time of year
March-May

Toilets ✓
Café (hot drinks and snacks only) ✓

The bittern is one of Britain's most elusive, secretive birds. A member of the heron family, unlike it's tall, grey, elegant cousin most people are familiar with, they are low, squat and skulk in the reedbeds they call home. In short, you hardly ever see them.

But, as with most birds, they do dispense with the secret spy act for the breeding season – males have got to find a female to mate with somehow – and they do it by making a noise that, depending on your point of view, either mimics a foghorn or the sound of someone blowing gently over the

---

DO IT YOURSELF

Ham Wall RSPB Reserve (BA6 9SX) is in the Somerset Levels between the villages of Meare to the north and Ashcott to the south, and there's a large visitor carpark. ✍ www.rspb.org/hamwall
☎ 01458 860494

Bitterns boom between roughly February and June, but peak months are March, April and May. They will boom all day, but morning or even first light is an excellent time to get there. There's a small, manned visitor centre which will be able to give you more information on where best to hear them.

top of a milk bottle. Personally, I'd say the latter. Most bird calls and songs are some kind of variation on the standard tweet, ranging from the raucous caw of a crow to the sweet singing of a song thrush, but the bittern's boom is something else.

I first heard one on a trip to Ham Wall, and I almost didn't notice it at first – it was lower and gentler than I'd been expecting while still being loud and carrying a remarkable distance over the open wetland. Oh, that's a boom, I thought. And then it was suddenly everywhere, as if there were four or five people hidden among the reeds, furtively playing the pan pipes.

This also is the one time that bitterns come out of their reedbed hidey-holes. Males boom to attract the females, but to seal the deal there's a courtship flight in which they lead her on a merry dance. Look for mottled-brown birds, their heads held out in front of them heron-style, their longish legs hanging down, I was told, but actual sightings eluded me.

Like deer stags, the male bittern's goal is to mate with as many females as possible. The boom not only attracts them but is also an indication of his fitness to breed and the quality of his genes – in order to do it properly, they must put on an additional 20 per cent of body weight purely into the muscles around their oesophagus, which they use to force air out and make that boom. It might not be a flash Lamborghini, but it's essentially the same idea.

56 HUNTING HOBBIES

SHAPWICK HEATH NNR

Family friendly ★★
Not easy to spot and almost impossible to predict if and when they'll be around

Budget friendly ★★★★
Small parking charges at Shapwick Heath

Amateur friendly ★★★
Relatively easy to identify – if you can find them

Best time of year
April-May

Toilets ✓
Cafe ✓

The hobby is a curious bird-of-prey to anyone other than a serious wildlife fanatic. Who knew they even existed? Where can you see them? And how did its scientific name lead to the name for an iconic children's game? More on that in a moment.

As a member of the falcon family, the hobby is related to birds such as peregrines (**Experience 21**) and kestrels (**Experience 35**), and has the

---

DO IT YOURSELF

Shapwick Heath (BA6 9TT) is a National Nature Reserve in the Somerset Levels.
⌀ avalonmarshes.org/explore/nature-reserves/shapwick-heath   ☎ 01458 860120

Cotswold Water Park is a large area of gravel pits north-west of Swindon. Contact CWP Trust for more information about possible hobby sightings in May and June. ⌀ www.waterpark.org/cwp-trust   ☎ 01793 752413

Hobbies can also be found in the New Forest. The National Park Authority recommends the damp heaths around Beaulieu Road Station in the early evening in May or early June.
⌀ www.newforestnpa.gov.uk/discover/wildlife/heathland-birds/hobby-2

same pointed, swept-back wing shape, rather than the blunter wings of a sparrowhawk. As every schoolboy knows, peregrines are the world's fastest animal thanks to its gravity-assisted stoops. Falcons in general are built for speed, so the same is true for hobbies. Unlike peregrines or kestrels, however, hobbies aren't resident in Britain – they only come here to breed for the spring and summer, and some are just passing through on their way to Scandinavia.

I've only seen hobbies once in my life, and it wasn't at Shapwick Heath, which is recognised as one of the best places to see them in Britain. I was at Cotswold Water Park, near Swindon – a much better wildlife spot than its proximity to the county town of Wiltshire suggests. But it was certainly a memorable experience, because hobbies are our only bird of prey that mainly hunt dragonflies and damselflies, and it makes for fascinating viewing.

I'd been out listening to nightingales in the early evening, and when we arrived at one of the lakes, a couple of hobbies were hurtling through the sky like feathered meteors, twisting this way and that in pursuit of a meal. Each time they grabbed a dragonfly or damselfly in mid-air, they'd then bring it up to their beak, feeding in mid-flight like an office worker gulping down a sandwich on the run.

And the children's game it inspired? The inventor of the classic football flick-fest, Subbuteo, was a birder, and he wanted a name for the new game he'd created. His favourite bird was the hobby, whose Latin name is *Falco subbuteo* – the rest, as they say, is history.

55 ROOSTING MARSH HARRIERS AND COMMON CRANES

STUBB MILL, HICKLING BROAD

Family friendly ★

Birds are mostly far away and you're standing around in the cold

Budget friendly ★★★★★

Nothing to pay – just bring a thermos

Amateur friendly ★★

Identifying raptors at a distance can be difficult

Best time of year

Dec-Feb

Toilets ✓

The best times of day for watching wildlife are frequently either the morning or the evening, when animals are either waking up and are hungry or looking for a place to

DO IT YOURSELF

Hickling Broad (NR12 0BW) is both a Norfolk Wildlife Trust reserve and National Nature Reserve – head for the car park on Stubb Road, just past the FAITH Animal Rescue centre. ⌂ www.norfolkwildlifetrust.org.uk/wildlife-in-norfolk/nature-reserves/reserves/hickling-broad ☎ 01603 625540

The way to Stubb Mill is not signposted. From the car park, you need to walk back up the road you've just driven down. Where the road bends sharply to the left, there is a track going to the right – that's the way to Stubb Mill. The track going straight on says Stubb Farm (so potentially confusing), but this isn't what you want. From this junction, it's about an 800 metre walk. There's a very slightly raised platform at the end of this track – to see the harriers and cranes, look mainly north and east.

Norfolk Wildlife Trust recommends arriving a good hour before sunset – in early December, that's as early as 2.30. Clear, still days are best.

sleep for the night. At Stubb Mill, you watch them go through their bedtime routine.

One of the things that's remarkable about this experience is that it involves two bird species that, until, 20 or 30 years ago, you'd have been lucky to see at all, let alone (in the case of the marsh harriers) such large numbers. They have only returned as reedbeds have been restored across the country, while cranes have come back as conservation groups have recreated the sort of wet, marshy habitat they prefer.

Some reports suggest you can see up to 90 marsh harriers here in a single evening, and 30 or 40 is not unusual – on my visit to Stubb Mill, a beautifully clear afternoon after a very wet and windy morning, I was able to count eight of these birds of prey at any one time.

They patrolled the huge expanse of rough grassland in front of me, perhaps looking for a final meal before calling it a night. One landed on a small hillock some 100 metres away, only to be ousted by a larger bird, a female, I presumed – they are often up to a third bigger than the males.

As the gloom deepened, I heard briefly and distantly cranes bugling, and later one pair, then a second, glided in on still wings and disappeared behind a small copse. There was just enough time before darkness fell to spot a beautiful grey male hen harrier with its distinctive black wingtips, a bird even rarer in England than the marsh harrier.

54 PURPLE EMPERORS

KNEPP ESTATE, HORSHAM

Family friendly ★ ★
Purple emperors can be elusive, and patience is required

Budget friendly ★ ★ ★
Guided walks at Knepp cost (in 2019) £45 per person

Amateur friendly ★ ★
Hard to find if you're not an expert, though they are distinctive butterflies

Best time of year
Adults emerge in late June through to early August – Knepp runs trips in early July

Like the swallowtail (**Experience 25**), the purple emperor – Britain's second-largest butterfly with a wingspan about as wide as the palm of your hand – hides a dark secret. The males, especially, may look stunning in all their purple finery, but beneath that regal beauty lie dirty desires – they absolutely love the foulest of smells, with rotting fish, stinking cheese and faeces of almost any description most irresistible. Some experts swear by urine-soaked fox scat to lure them out of their treetop haunts.

DO IT YOURSELF

Knepp Estate (RH13 8NN) runs expert-led, purple emperor butterfly safaris in July. ☎ 01403 713 230 ⌨ www.kneppsafaris.co.uk

Bentley Wood on the Hampshire/Wiltshire border is renowned as a place to see purple emperors. ⌨ www.purple-emperor.co.uk/bentley-wood

Fermyn Woods, in Northamptonshire, is also good. ⌨ www.northamptonshireparks.co.uk/fermyn-woods-country-park/Pages/default.aspx

Males naturally spend a lot of their time high in an oak woodland canopy, where they feed on tree sap and aphid honeydew, but they also like to come down to the ground to probe for salts or minerals in animal dung – other smelly substances appear to perform the same trick.

Females, which though not purple are still a beautiful dark brown, lay their eggs in thickets of sallow, also known as pussy or goat willow, because the caterpillars feed on their leaves, so males also patrol these shrubs in search of a mate.

Until recently, purple emperors were a Holy Grail for butterfly nerds only – there's a well-known location on the Hampshire/Wiltshire border and another in Northamptonshire, but for anyone with only a passing interest or little expertise, there was little easily accessible information on where to find them.

But now there's a place which has become astonishingly good for the species in the past decade – Knepp Estate, a few miles south of Horsham, now recognised as having the largest population in the whole of Britain.

How this happened is a story in itself – since early 2000, Knepp owners Charlie Burrell and Isabella Tree have turned the 1,400ha estate (which has been in the Burrell family since the early 1800s) over to nature under a process called rewilding.

There are a number of interpretations of rewilding, but in the case of Knepp, Charlie and Isabella have largely left what was traditional arable farmland and pasture to run wild. Their only intervention has been to introduce a small number of herbivores – longhorn cattle, Tamworth pigs, red and fallow deer and Exmoor ponies – which help drive habitat restoration.

The result – at Knepp, anyway – has been a proliferation of sallow scrub that the purple emperors need for their caterpillars, and hence the boom in numbers of the species itself.

53 FEEDING COAL AND CRESTED TITS

LOCH GARTEN RSPB RESERVE, CAIRNGORMS NATIONAL PARK

Family friendly ★★★★★

A great one for children – very little patience or hardship required

Budget friendly ★★★★★

Just bring a bag of sunflower hearts – entrance to the reserve is free

Amateur friendly ★★★★★

Yes, but learn to tell the difference between coal tits and crested tits – the former have the black caps, the latter the mohicans

Best time of year

All year round

Toilets ✓

Generally speaking, wildlife experts discourage actual contact with wild animals. They can carry diseases that they could potentially pass onto you (and vice versa) and hugging or holding one against its will is not generally regarded as a great idea. But in the carpark at the Abernethy-Loch Garten RSPB Reserve – just a stone's throw from Loch Garten itself on one side and the osprey hide (**Experience 24**) on the other – our leading bird conservation charity actively encourages you to do just that. So, if you ask me, make the most of it – all you need is a bag of sunflower hearts.

DO IT YOURSELF

Loch Garten RSPB Reserve (PH25 3EF) is in the north-west of the Cairngorms and about 10km outside of Aviemore (the main tourist centre of the national park). ✆ www.rspb.org/lochgarten
☎ 01479 831476

Apart from coal and crested tits, and ospreys in the spring and summer, you've also got a very good chance of seeing red squirrels here.

This is essentially the same as feeding your garden birds, except these have become so habituated to people they are entirely comfortable taking the food out of your hand, and instead of blue tits and great tits, which are the two species most people are likely to find on their feeders, you'll mainly see coal and crested tits.

Coal tits are lovely little birds, with a smart black cap and bib on their throat, a greyish back and buffy underparts, and they'll have clocked you the moment you get out of your car. Feeding them is really very simple – put a quantity of hearts in the palm of your hand and wait. It won't take long.

But it's the crested tits – or cresties, as serious birders like to call them – that many people come for. Though common in regions such as Scandinavia, in Britain, they're only found in a smallish area of northern Scotland (with the pine forests of the Cairngorms being their stronghold), so they're generally a less familiar species. In colouration, they're quite similar to the coal tits (just with a brown not slate-grey back), but they're bigger and easily identified by the very splendid, punk hair-do from which they get their name.

Despite this rather cocky look, on my visit to Abernethy they were definitely less bold than the coal tits, which were feeding out of everyone's hands almost constantly. Hence, I got a great picture of a coal tit, but a rather ropy one of a crestie.

52 BLUEBELLS

ANCIENT DECIDUOUS WOODLAND

Family Friendly ★★
Beautiful as they are, bluebells may not be the greatest hit with children

Budget Friendly ★★★★★
Bluebell woods are mainly free

Amateur friendly ★★★★★
One of our most distinctive wildflowers

Best time of year
April-May

DO IT YOURSELF

The Wildlife Trusts has a list of 100 locations in England and Wales that are good for bluebells – of those mentioned, I can vouch for Siccaridge Woods in Gloucestershire and Folly Farm, south of Bristol in Bath and North East Somerset (the old county of Avon). ⌐ www.wildlifetrusts.org/dazzled-by-bluebells ☎ 01636 677711

BBC Wildlife has recommendations from both wildlife organisations and its readers on its website. ⌐ www.discoverwildlife.com/british-wildlife/see-it/top-places-see-bluebells

The Woodland Trust has a list of 10 of its own reserves that are bluebell havens. ⌐ www.woodlandtrust.org.uk/blog/2015/04/top-10-bluebell-woods ☎ 01476 581111

The trust also has a handy guide to distinguishing our native bluebells from invasive Spanish ones – most bluebells in urban areas are probably the latter.

The most unusual place I know for bluebells is Skomer Island off the west coast of Pembrokeshire – here they don't grow in woodland but out in the open. Details of how to get to Skomer from the Wildlife Trust of South and West Wales. ⌐ www.welshwildlife.org/skomer-skokholm/skomer ☎ 01656 724100

A point made by David Attenborough in his 1995 TV series *The Life of Plants* is that there's a reason why the British Isles are the best place in the world to see bluebells – at the end of the last Ice Age, the ice retreated, allowing animals and plants from mainland Europe to colonise our previously icy wastes, but then the land bridge was quickly cut off by rising sea levels. Only a relatively small number of plant species made it, so those that did now face less competition.

As a result, bluebells carpet woodland floors here in a way they cannot on mainland Europe, and so the spectacle is correspondingly greater. Indeed, according to the Woodland Trust, half the world's entire population of bluebells grows in the UK, making it truly impossible to name just one place to find them – there are so many, there's probably not a single county in the country that doesn't have at least one fabulous location.

More even perhaps than wild garlic (**Experience 99**), bluebells *en masse* play a trick, an optical illusion, on the viewer – single, delicate flowerheads coalesce into a purple (let's be honest, the flower is badly named) haze that seems to shimmer like a mirage.

You can chance on them anywhere. Cycling through quiet country lanes north of Gloucester in late April, I entered the tiny village of Upleadon and passed one of those bluebell woodlands that makes you drop everything and just gawp. I wouldn't necessarily recommend anyone drove all the way to Upleadon to see this for themselves (the residents might not thank me), but it just goes to show you can stumble across them anywhere.

51 SEABIRD CITY

THE SHIANT ISLES, OUTER HEBRIDES

Family friendly ★
The Shiant Isles are difficult to get to, and the only shelter is a shepherd's hut

Budget friendly ★
Expensive to get there

Amateur friendly ★★★★
Guillemots, puffins and razorbills are all easy to identify

Best time of year
April-July

The Shiant Isles are a small archipelago of three main islands some 8km off the east coast of Harris in the Outer Hebrides. They are uninhabited and used to be owned by the writer Adam Nicolson until he gave them to his son, Tom.

DO IT YOURSELF

More information about the Shiant Isles: ✆ www.shiantisles.net – you can contact Tom Nicolson by email: tom@shiantisles.net

One of the other great 'seabird cities' is the Isle of May in the Firth of Forth. Scotland's National Nature Reserves ✆ www.nature.scot/enjoying-outdoors/scotlands-national-nature-reserves/isle-may-national-nature-reserve

To visit, try Anstruther Pleasure Trips (✆ www.isleofmayferry.com ☎ 07957 585200) or Isle of May Boat Trips (✆ www.isleofmayboattrips.co.uk ☎ 07473 631671).

A four-year project to remove black rats from the Shiant Isles to increase the seabirds' breeding success began in 2014. Visitors to the islands are asked to make sure they don't have rats on their boat, or if they do, they don't land or indeed push rats overboard (they swim rather well). ✆ www.rspb.org/shiantisles ☎ 01859 550463.

I've been there once. On a cruise that had promised to take me to St Kilda, we were boxed in by the weather and forced to hole up in the harbour of East Loch Tarbert for a day while the storm dissipated. Realising we no longer had time to get to St Kilda, our skipper decided on the next best thing – the Shiants.

We circled round the north side of Garbh Eilean (Rough Island), which is joined by a narrow isthmus to another island of a similar size and known as Eilean an Taighe (House Island). Behind us was a third island, creating an enclosed bay where hundreds of birds flew over our heads and gathered in rafts on the water. Guillemots and razorbills nested on the coal-black basalt of Rough Island – which is made up of angular columns reminiscent of Fingal's Cave on Staffa – and though it's an overused comparison, it was hard not to think of this huge seabird colony as being like one of our own cities, its residents going about their daily business and gathering food for hungry families.

Indeed, according to the most recent estimates, some 100,000 pairs of seabirds breed here during the summer months, including more than 60,000 pairs of puffins, representing about 10 per cent of the entire UK population.

We dropped anchor and set out in a small dinghy to land on the shingle isthmus. Adam Nicolson recommends you watch the birds from a boat and then go for a walk on House Island, leaving those nesting on Rough Island undisturbed. The odds are that, apart from whoever you came with, you'll be completely alone, with just the cries of the seabirds and the roar of the wind to keep you company.

50 TRAIL CAMERA PHOTOGRAPHY

ANY BACK GARDEN

Family friendly ★★★★★
Great fun for children of all ages

Budget friendly ★★
Expect to pay at least £140 for a trail cam – and up to £350 if you get serious

Amateur friendly ★★★★
Easy to use and the chances are you'll snap deer, foxes and badgers, none of which should tax your ID skills unduly

Best time of year
All year round

Trail cameras (or trailcams, for short) are great pieces of kit made possible by the digital photography revolution. You can put them up anywhere in theory, though most people tend to stick them in their back garden to see what wildlife great and small is using it as a thoroughfare or feeding ground under cover of the night.

The premise is very simple: if the sensor detects something moving, it takes a picture (or video, if you want). Memory cards these days are sufficiently

DO IT YOURSELF

The best, cheap trailcams on the market are made by Bushnell. It has a range of models of different specifications that start at about £140, but have a good look round different online retailers, because prices (for the same model) can vary wildly. 🖰 www.bushnell.eu ☎ 0208 391 4700

Other trailcam makes on the market include Stealthcam (🖰 https://www.bushwear.co.uk/brands/stealthcam) and Browning (🖰 https://www.trail-tech.co.uk/product-category/cameras/browning). I used an early version of Stealthcam some years ago (and it was fine), but I have no recent knowledge of either of these manufacturers.

large to be able to store thousands of images, so you can leave the camera for a week or more, clicking away, then download the pictures whenever you want.

It's fun taking pictures of foxes, badgers, the occasional roe or muntjac deer and early morning magpies and jackdaws, though you do end up trawling through an awful lot of pictures of the local cat population or where some branches have moved in the wind. But as with many things in life, it's panning the gold from the alluvial deposit that is half the fun of it. For just over a year, I had a camera on a local river that I was monitoring for non-native mink, and it took endless pictures of the swirling current, debris in the water or the local mallard ducks.

There was often so much chaff, indeed, I'd got to the point where I was just going 'delete', 'delete', 'delete' without really thinking, so it totally took me by surprise when the sinuous form of an otter appeared. An otter! In a sleepy village in Gloucestershire on a river that never appears to be especially rich in wildlife.

But then, it just goes to show how wrong you can be. At one point, my camera was taking a picture of an otter – the same one I assume – three or four times a week, and soon I was also finding their spraints (a fancy word for otter poo) on almost every visit, and I concluded they were going up and down the river on a regular basis.

49 WILLOW WARBLERS

DUNNET HEAD RSPB RESERVE, NEAR THURSO

Family friendly ★
Probably hard to get children excited by this

Budget friendly ★★★★
A very remote part of Britain, but otherwise free

Amateur friendly ★★★
Some people struggle with birdsong, but the willow warbler is quite an easy one to learn

Best time of year
April-June

Two of our most distinctive migrant songbirds are the chiffchaff and the willow warbler. They overwinter in Africa (though some chiffchaffs now don't bother because it's sufficiently warm in Britain these days), returning in March and April and taking over our woodlands and hedgerows for a few months.

I say they're distinctive songbirds – in fact, they are nondescript, near-identical, olive-brown warblers that can be hard to spot at all among the foliage. No, it's their songs I'm talking about – the willow warbler's a lovely, joyful trill of cascading notes, the other a metronomic, two-note ditty that I would struggle to call beautiful but is certainly unique. For me, it's the chiffchaff's song, which I usually first hear around mid-March, that truly heralds the onset of spring.

DO IT YOURSELF

Dunnet Head RSPB Reserve (KW14 8XS) is very easy to find. ✆ www.rspb.org/dunnethead ☎ 01463 715000

It's mainly a small seabird colony, and home to puffins, guillemots, razorbills, kittiwakes and fulmars.

Both birds have a massive global range and are theoretically found throughout Britain, but on a bike ride from the south coast of Devon to the British mainland's northernmost point – not John O'Groats, as it happens, but Dunnet Head, a little to the west – I found it was a bit more complex than that.

Starting at Dawlish Warren, at the mouth of the River Exe, I cycled through Devon, Somerset, Gloucestershire, Worcestershire, Staffordshire and into Cheshire, and during that time chiffchaffs hugely outnumbered willow warblers. By the time I'd reached Lancashire, they were about equal in numbers, but once I was in Scotland, I heard mainly willow warblers and very few chiffchaffs. On quiet, country lanes, I'd sometimes hear a different willow warbler every 50 or 100m. It was as if they were willing me on.

I started to wonder where would I hear my last willow warbler, and on my final day, after trundling east from Thurso, I eventually reached the mini peninsula of Dunnet Head, a windswept thumb of land sticking out into the North Atlantic in the direction of Orkney.

Here, farmland slowly gives way to peaty lochans and stands of gorse – not the most compelling habitat for these birds – and, yet, on a gorse bush just a few hundred metres from the very edge of Britain, there was a willow warbler, singing its heart out just ten metres or so from me. It's probably the best view I've had of this bird in my life.

I can't prove, of course, it was mainland Britain's most northerly songbird, but given after that there was just the cliffs of Dunnet Head, a few hundred seabirds and the vast swell of the North Atlantic, you'd have been hard-pressed to find another.

48 HUNTING BARN OWLS

LAKENHEATH FEN RSPB RESERVE, SUFFOLK

Family friendly ★★

Exciting to see but fairly unpredictable – being up at dawn improves your chances

Budget friendly ★★★★

Car park costs £4 for non-members

Amateur friendly ★★★

The pale form of a barn owl is hard to mistake for anything else, but a certain amount of expertise required to find them

Best time of year

All year round – though your chances of seeing one in daylight increase on cold, calm days

Toilets ✓

We'd been watching marsh harriers hunting over the reedbeds when someone suddenly shouted: 'Barn owl!' Sure enough, less than 100 metres away, there it was, quartering a rough area of grass, clearly on the look-out for a voley snack or two. It was late-April, so there's a chance it already had a partner sitting on eggs or even chicks to feed.

It flew back and forth in a jerky fashion, not quite hovering like a kestrel but not a speed merchant like a peregrine or sparrowhawk either. Its ghostly appearance and idiosyncratic flying style meant it was something you could identify almost without thinking.

DO IT YOURSELF

Lakenheath Fen RSPB Reserve (IP27 9AD) is just to the west of Thetford Forest Park, and the nearest large town is Thetford. It runs a wide variety of guided walks, including ones specifically for barn owls. ✆ www.rspb.org/lakenheathfen ☎ 01842 863400

Ham Wall RSPB Reserve (BA6 9SX) in Somerset is also good. ✆ www.rspb.org/hamwall ☎ 01458 860494

Then, it dropped, no more than about ten metres, down to the ground and out of view from our position in the hide. We tried moving, but the owl had gone, and when it didn't reappear after a minute or two, we turned our attention back to those marsh harriers.

As with all barn owl encounters I've ever had, it came without warning. Watching them hunt is very special, but some of my most memorable sightings have been while driving at dusk or night, their ghostly forms almost glowing in the headlights.

By virtue of being largely nocturnal, most owls are largely unknown to us. Many people will hear the classic 'Whoo-hoo' of tawny owls (**Experience 64**) from time to time if they live in relatively rural locations and will probably recognise, but rarely have seen for themselves, the heart-shaped face and snowy white breast feathers of a barn owl. What's truly remarkable about this bird is just how widespread it is – it's found on six out of seven of the world's continents (just not Antarctica) and from China to Chile.

Here in the UK, it lives a fragile existence – intensification of farming after the Second World War led to rough pastures being ploughed up and planted and the disappearance of prey such as voles, while conversion of agricultural barns into homes resulted in a loss of nesting sites. In some areas, conservation efforts have helped to turn the barn owl's fortunes around, but in much of the country they are either very rare or entirely absent. Regional hotspots include large parts of East Anglia and the Somerset Levels.

47 SNORKEL TRAIL

KIMMERIDGE BAY

Family friendly ★★★

Easy snorkelling in shallow water – a 12-year-old child who's a confident swimmer could do it

Budget friendly ★★★★

Just the cost of a mask and snorkel – or hire them for £5

Amateur friendly ★★★★

Staff at the marine centre can give you tips on how to identify fish and seaweed

Best time of year

June-August

Toilets ✓

Wearing a short summer wetsuit and neoprene shoes, I waded into the gently shelving limestone seabed of Kimmeridge Bay. Once it was up to my waist, I positioned my mask and snorkel and took the plunge. Even though it was July during a heatwave, the chilly water was still a shock to the system, and it was a while before I could relax in my new environment.

Once I did, I began to take in my surroundings. Bootlace seaweed grew up from the seabed in long, black strands that were covered in what resembled a

DO IT YOURSELF

The snorkel trail was developed by Dorset Wildlife Trust, and is overseen by its Fine Foundation Wild Seas Centre. Staff at the centre can hire out masks and snorkels and give advice as to the suitability of conditions in the bay (including on the best tide state), but they don't lead swimmers in the water. Definitely worth calling a few days in advance if you can. 🖱 www.dorsetwildlifetrust. org.uk/snorkelling_trail.html ☎ 01929 481044

Even in summer, I'd recommend wearing a wetsuit and neoprene shoes, but the wildlife trust advises against (and you really don't need) fins. Conditions are much better if it's been calm the few days before you do the trail.

thick white film (but which turned out to be tiny hairs), and beautiful golden wireweed with its delicate fronds waved in the gentle current.

Almost immediately, I saw a fish, then another – two corkwing wrasse about six inches long, easily identifiable from the black spots just in front of their tails. If this makes me sound like I know what I'm talking about, I don't (or, at least, I didn't); I'd had some tips from staff at the marine centre, where they also have handy laminated ID cards that you can take on the trail if you wish.

Next, I saw some much smaller fish that I took to be blennies and a couple of brown, or edible, crabs about as big as my hand – that would be small by this species' standards, but in any case, there's no foraging for your supper on this trail. It's purely about the experience.

Best of all was a couple of ballan wrasse, large fish that looked almost half a metre long which I ran into when I reached deeper water. They skirted around the seaweed fronds, eyeing me up with suspicion before disappearing into the forest of vegetation.

I meandered along the course, which is really just a zig-zag series of five buoys, for about an hour – I've always thought snorkelling just about one of the most relaxing things you can do, and the experience in the UK may be less exhilarating than a tropical coral reef, but in many ways no less rewarding.

46 KONIK PONIES

WICKEN FEN

Family friendly ★★★★
Kids love ponies – these just happen to be wild (or nearly wild)

Budget friendly ★★★
Entry to Wicken Fen will cost about £20 for a family of four

Amateur friendly ★★★★★
Most people know a horse when they see one

Best time of year
All year round

Toilets ✓
Cafe ✓

'So, I think we'd better just move over here,' Wicken Fen ranger Maddie Downes said to me, as it became clear that the space in which we were standing was about to be occupied. The konik ponies were coming our way.

There were some 40 of them, split into small groups consisting of one stallion, several mares and their offspring. I could see individuals jostling for position, and there was a pungent smell of horse in the air. It felt wild and

---

DO IT YOURSELF

Wicken Fen (CB7 5XP) is a national nature reserve, managed and partly owned by the National Trust, north-east of Cambridge.

The bigger, breeding group of konik ponies is found on Baker's Fen, which can be easily accessed by foot or on bike (you can hire bikes there), and maps of Wicken Fen are available at the reception area.

The trust offers occasional guided ranger or extensive grazing walks. See the website for details:
🖱 www.nationaltrust.org.uk/wicken-fen-nature-reserve ☎ 01353 720274

feral, and in the cooling September afternoon and surrounded by the expanse of the fen, the sight of a cave bear or woolly mammoth lumbering out of the woods wouldn't have been out of place.

There are no truly wild horses anywhere in Britain or Europe. Even those that appear to live wild, such as those found on Dartmoor, are semi-feral versions of domesticated animals. They're hardy, yes, but not wild. The same is largely true of konik ponies, but they're special in a couple of ways.

First, with their dun (light-brown) coats, black dorsal stripes along their backs and stripes on their lower legs, they are said to resemble the tarpan, the extinct European wild horse. Second, they're so tough they can be left to fend for themselves with almost no intervention, and they live on the fen all year round.

Wicken Fen is a large area of grassland and fenland (typically a wet, marshy area dominated by sedges) that the National Trust has great plans for – it wants to turn more than 50km^2 into true wilderness over the course of this century, and one of the ways it is doing this is by maintaining the open grassland with the use of the ponies. Otherwise, it would scrub up and turn into woodland, leading to the loss of species associated with the fen.

The ponies came over to us, the youngsters with curious and edgy energy. They crowded around, but soon lost interest and wandered away. Wild or not, they're still a fascinating throwback to an ancient past.

45 EXTREME CRABBING

NEW QUAY, CEREDIGION

Family friendly ★★★★★
Children love this new take on an old favourite

Budget friendly ★★
2017 prices were £15 per person, £10 for children under 12, for a 1½ hour trip – potentially £50 for a family of four.

Amateur friendly ★★★★★
Just don't get nipped

Best time of year
A summer activity – May-Sept

Toilets ✓

Most people don't need a book to tell them crabbing can be fun or how and where to do it. But there's crabbing – and then there's *crabbing*, and no one does it better, in my experience, than Tim and Corinne Harrison in New Quay in the heart of Cardigan Bay.

For a start, you're not standing on a pier or quayside, but you chug out into the sheltered bay just beyond the town's harbour walls on a boat. Then you drop specially designed crabbing nets, baited with mackerel chum, into the depths and – just like any normal crabbing escapade – you wait.

Naturally, our children pulled up the nets, against Tim's advice, far too soon and were disappointed to find we'd caught nothing, so we dropped them down again and this time they showed some patience. And once they'd got into the swing of this waiting game, we started to unlock the treasures of the deep.

DO IT YOURSELF

Epic Fishing's 'Captain's Crab' trips last for 1½ hours. You don't need any equipment yourself, just warm and waterproof clothes and a supply of food and water. There's a loo on board the boat, but not much else. ⌖ www.bassfishingtrips.co.uk ☎ 07989 496526

First a crab, but it looked quite distinct from any I'd seen before. It had a rough, furry brown carapace the size of a child's hand, purply pincers and fierce red eyes that suggest it's got a vicious little nip (which apparently it has) – a velvet swimming crab.

Next, some came some glassy prawns, a baby pouting, which we named Tiddler in honour of the eponymous book by *The Gruffalo* author Julia Donaldson, and a few greeny shore crabs, the ones you normally catch while doing it off the pier. Then, the catch of the day, a small, but perfectly formed dark blue lobster, waving its pincers energetically at its captors as if challenging us all to a fight.

All the catches were temporarily housed in a bucket for the children and adults to admire. Then Tim suddenly got very excited with something that had caught his eye in one of the nets and began to sift through what looked like just a mass of seaweed. 'If this is what I think it is…' he was muttering to himself. We stood around, wondering what Tim could have found, when in front of our eyes, part of the seaweed morphed into the shape of a tiny crab.

'There,' said Tim, 'Do you see it? It's a baby spider crab – they stick seaweed on their shells for camouflage.' In my experience, you're unlikely to catch one of those with a weighted line and a packet of bacon.

44 CHURRING NIGHTJARS

WESTLETON HEATH NNR, NEAR MINSMERE

Family friendly ★★
Not really – hearing nightjars requires staying up until it's dark in late spring/early summer

Budget friendly ★★★★
Even guided walks are cheap

Amateur friendly ★★★
The churring call of a nightjar is like nothing else

Best time of year
May-June

Until I made this trip to Westleton Heath, a National Nature Reserve (NNR) that (as its name suggests) is a heathland of low scrubby plants and bushes that include various species of heather, I'd only ever seen and heard nightjars in sub-Saharan Africa. They were different species to the ones we get here, but most nightjars make the distinctive churring noise that I associated with dusty tropical landscapes, red soil and hot, humid evenings.

My first thought was that nightjars would feel somehow too exotic for this British landscape and an evening of relative cool that held no promise

---

DO IT YOURSELF

Minsmere RSPB Reserve runs regular nightjar experience evenings during the summer (May & June). ⌐ www.rspb.org/minsmere ☎ 01728 648281

Norfolk is also a good area for nightjars – contact Norfolk Wildlife Trust. ⌐ www.norfolkwildlifetrust.org.uk/wildlife-in-norfolk/species-explorer/birds/nightjar ☎ 01603 625540

The heathlands of South Dorset are another hotspot, and Arne RSPB Reserve (BH20 5BJ) runs nightjar events. ⌐ www.rspb.org/arne ☎ 01929 553360

of sunbaked African heat. It had been a mixed day of some sunshine and occasional strong, blustery squalls in early June, but by the time dusk was approaching around 9pm, it had quietened down and was clear if not completely still.

With the RSPB's Louise Gregory, I walked a short circuit of Westleton Heath, just north of the village of Westleton. Just as it was getting dark, around 9.30, the first nightjar started up, a regular, insect-like sound that would be easy to confuse with a cicada or grasshopper – indeed according to some sources, it is very similar to the European mole cricket (though, I confess, that doesn't help me especially).

The song – if you can call it a song – is meant to be both a territorial 'Keep out!' to other males, as well as a 'Come on!' to any females in the area. Soon Louise had identified three or four males in our vicinity. On a good day, she said, nightjars can be heard 600m away. We only rarely saw any birds – occasionally flying above our heads, then later one sitting characteristically on a tree, its body flattened against the branch and beautifully camouflaged. The constant churring was soothing and almost soporific – a decent recording could be an excellent aid for insomniacs.

Nightjars are part of a large group of birds called Caprimulgiformes, which means 'goat-suckers' because of the belief that they drank milk from the teats of female goats. In fact, they hunt moths and other flying insects, and though they feed predominantly at dusk, they nevertheless rely on their eyesight to catch their prey, which they can see silhouetted against the sky.

43 ORCHIDS AND OTHER WILDFLOWERS

CLATTINGER FARM, COTSWOLD WATER PARK

Family friendly ★★★
Pleasant, easy walking in flower-filled fields

Budget friendly ★★★★★
Another free adventure

Amateur friendly ★★★
If you're not bothered about identifying different orchid species, just enjoy the giddy floral displays

Best time of year
May-July

© James Fair.

Adisplay of wild orchids is a sight to lift the soul, and I can't think of a better place than Clattinger Farm on a sunny, late spring afternoon. In my experience, mid-May to early June is the best time to go because

DO IT YOURSELF

Clattinger Farm (SN6 9TW) is owned and managed by Wiltshire Wildlife Trust. ⌁ www. wiltshirewildlife.org/lower-moor-farm-including-clattinger-farm-sandpool-oaksey-moor-farm-meadow-cricklade   ☎ 01380 725670

There are two ways to access Clattinger Farm. The trust's website takes you to Lower Moor Farm on Spine Road West, and from here you can walk up into Clattinger Farm along a track and then footpaths. But you can also access the farm from the (unnamed) road that heads south from Spine Road West at the Neigh Bridge Country Park crossroads. Drive down here about 1km, and there is a style on the right-hand side (with a sign and interpretation board). There is very little parking here, however.

There's an excellent selection of 40 wildflower meadows, from Cornwall to Cumbria (taking in Wales and many counties in between) on the *Country Life* website: ⌁ www.countrylife.co.uk/news/visit-the-best-wildflower-meadows-in-the-uk-24278

you've still got some of the butter-yellow cowslips running riot, but also a rich profusion of richly purple green-winged orchids together with other species of a pinker, paler hue.

This is an experience, which requires you to fully re-engage with Mother Earth. You can't just wander round admiring the colours, you must get down on your hands and knees, or even your front, to get the full spectacle. From six feet or so above the ground, the flowers seem quaint and pretty, but down at their level, they become living, breathing, sexy beasts.

There are several fields here, and an obvious path taking you round the perimeter of them (don't go trampling across them), and this will give you plenty of close-up contact with the rich diversity of blooms. Look out too for the army of bumblebees, hoverflies and butterflies that must pollinate the plants. From ground level, you also get an idea of the tangle of life, not just the showy orchids but the grasses and hawkweeds growing tall and spindly as they reach for the light.

Clattinger Farm is described as a 'traditional hay meadow', and the reason it's so special is because the previous owners (and the current one, Wiltshire Wildlife Trust) have never used any artificial fertilisers to aid the growth of the grass. It means that flowers – the cowslips and orchids and many others – that live there naturally have not been crowded out by grasses that would, if given artificial help, outcompete them. This type of habitat would once have been common across the whole of lowland England, but today there are less than 15,000ha left in the UK.

42 WILD BOAR

FOREST OF DEAN

Family friendly ★★★★
'We're going on a boar hunt!'

Budget friendly ★★★★
You might have to pay for
parking, but otherwise free

Amateur friendly ★★★
Recognising field signs of boar
require some expertise, boar
themselves are unmissable

Best time of year
All year round

Toilets ✓
Cafe ✓

'I'm just going to dive round the back of that thicket,' Gareth said. 'There's a boar in there somewhere, and I reckon I can flush it out.'

'Righto', 'Great', and 'Is that really such a good idea?' I thought, but didn't try to stop him. Though I'd only met Gareth for the first time about two hours earlier, he seemed to know what he was doing, but he was nevertheless planning to sneak up on an animal weighing up to 100kg

DO IT YOURSELF

Wild boar may be found almost anywhere in the Forest of Dean, but one area you could try is woodland surrounding the Sculpture Trail, just to the east of Coleford. ᵛᵗ www.forestofdean-sculpture.org.uk ☎ 0300 067 4800

You'll have a better chance of seeing wild boar if you go either at first light or late afternoon/dusk. There's a lot more information about wild boar on the British Wild Boar website ᵛᵗ www.britishwildboar.org.uk

Though large and bulky animals, wild boar are not dangerous to people. But be sensible (as you would with any wildlife of the same size) – keep a safe distance from them, especially if they are females with piglets.

and that can run at 40kph – rather him than me was my over-riding emotion.

So, Gareth disappeared into the thicket, and after a few minutes, there was some brief rustling in the stand of young pine trees and out shot an animal that looked as big as a Shetland pony. Unmistakably pig-like, but dark, hairy and somewhat menacing, it bolted across the track some 10 of 15 metres from where I was standing and disappeared into a similar thicket on the other side.

It's believed that wild boar went extinct in Britain in the thirteenth century and were absent from our countryside for the next 700 years or so. Then farming them for their meat started here in the 1980s, and though it's not clear exactly when animals began escaping (or being deliberately released) into the countryside, by 1998, they were well and truly back.

There are number of populations all around Britain, but the Forest of Dean has the most substantial one. It's probably fair to say they divide opinion; some locals blame them for digging up their lawns and chasing dogs, while many others feel we should welcome them as part of our natural fauna.

There's also a fair bit of disagreement about how many there are, with population estimates beginning at around 800. That doesn't mean they're easy to see, but signs of their presence are everywhere, once you know what they are.

First, look for where they have dug up turf, which can be seen throughout the forest, most easily by the roadsides. It looks similar to what badgers do to garden lawns, but on an industrial scale. Then there are their droppings, which are black, quite large and irregularly shaped. Footprints are the classic cloven hoof shape also left by deer, but you'd need to be skilled to tell the two apart.

41 DIVE-BOMBING TERNS

THE FARNE ISLANDS

Family friendly ★★★★
This is a great trip for children, with lots of other birds besides terns to see, plus seals too

Budget friendly ★★
A 2½ hour trip will cost about £50-60 for a family of four, with landing on Inner Farne another £25 (National Trust members land for free)

Amateur friendly ★★★★
Terns are easy to recognise – blood red bills and feet, black caps, angel's wings and the devil's cry

Best time of year
Late May-August

Toilets (on Inner Farne) ✓
Café (on Inner Farne) ✓

Most wild animals in the UK run, fly or swim away when people are nearby. On the whole, they're nervous of us humans and with good reason, and while there are always exceptions, there are particular birds that go out of their way to hound us if we get anywhere near them – and they're the size of jackdaws and weigh no more than a bar of soap.

DO IT YOURSELF

The Farne Islands are owned by the National Trust. ⌂ www.nationaltrust.org.uk/farne-islands ☎ 01289 389244

Four separate boat companies run trips to the Farne Islands: ☎ Billy Shiel (01665 720308), Golden Gate (01665 721819), Serenity (01665 721667) and St Cuthbert (01665 720388) Details of all of them here: ⌂ www.nationaltrust.org.uk/farne-islands/features/getting-to-the-farnes. All boats leave from Seahouses.

If you prefer not to be dive-bombed, you can take a trip that only lands on Staple Island, and watch the terns plunge-diving from the boat.

But then Arctic terns are special birds in all sorts of ways. They complete a half circumnavigation of the globe every six months, spending the summer months breeding mainly in the Arctic (and as far south as Britain), then travelling to the Antarctic for our winter to get the best of the good climate down under. One Arctic tern was found to have travelled 96,000km in one year. It's said they see more sunlight than any other creature.

The Farne Islands are one of the best places in Britain to see these feisty fiends, with some 1,200 pairs nesting on the island of Inner Farne. Trips from Seahouses first take you round Staple Island to admire the dapper guillemots and razorbills, before landing on Inner Farne.

If you're there any time from late May until mid-August, however, be extremely careful where you go on Inner Farne and wear a soft hat – the terns regard you as a threat to their eggs or chicks, which may be very close to the paths, and will dive-bomb you, even pecking at your head (they've been known to draw blood) and calling out in a manic, high-pitched screech.

In fact, on my only trip to the Farne Islands, it was early May and the terns hadn't arrived back yet. But when I went to Westray, in the Orkney Islands, with my family one August, we discovered a small colony of breeding Arctic terns on the rocky shore between Mae Sand and the Bay of Tuquoy, in the south-west of the island. We watched them screeching at the wind and fishing off Mae Sand from a safe distance – and without the crowds you get on the Farnes.

40 DRAGONS' DEN

CORS DYFI NATURE RESERVE, MACHYNLLNETH, POWYS

Family friendly ★★★★★
Close-up encounters with common lizards

Budget friendly ★★★★
Except for members of Montgomeryshire Wildlife Trust, there's a small charge to enter the reserve – £3 for an adult, free for children under 16

Amateur friendly ★★★★★
The lizards are easy to spot and recognise

Best time of year
June-August

Toilets ✓
Cafe ✓

We only stopped because my partner understands a smattering of Welsh. 'Dyfi Osprey Project!' she shrieked where I saw a meaningless assortment of consonants and 'Y's. We pulled into a small

---

DO IT YOURSELF

Cors Dyfi Nature Reserve (SY20 8SR) is located just off the A487 between Machynlleth and Aberystwyth, and it's open from 10am to 6pm daily. ⌐⊕ www.montwt.co.uk/reserves/cors-dyfi ☎ 01654 781414

The best time to see common lizards is from April to September. You're more likely to see them on the boardwalk if the sun is out.

According to the Amphibian and Reptile Conservation Trust, common lizards can be seen through-out Britain, most frequently on 'commons, heaths, moorland, dry stone walls, embankments and sea cliffs', and they can grow to a maximum of 15cm long. ⌐⊕ www.arc-trust.org/common-lizard ☎ 01202 391319

carpark even as I wondered out loud whether, as it was late August, the ospreys wouldn't have already begun their migration back to West Africa.

But the friendly Montgomeryshire Wildlife Trust staff assured us the male and his offspring were still here. In fact, you could see him on a live webcam, standing beside the now vacated nest, and it was a short walk on a boardwalk to get to the hide.

Our children were lukewarm about the prospect of seeing ospreys, but when I noticed the tiny dragon basking by the side of the boardwalk, their spirits perked up – miniature wildlife close-up is always a bigger attraction for young children than large animals a long way off. The first ones we saw were small and dark, just a few centimetres long, and seemingly unafraid of us.

They were common lizards, one of three lizard species naturally found in the British Isles – the other two being the confusingly named slow worm (it's not a worm – and even though it doesn't have legs, it's not a snake) and the sand lizard, which is very rare in this country.

Soon we were seeing them every few yards. The tiny younger ones had almost jet black tails that looked as if they'd been scorched in a furnace, but as they get older, they lose that dragony look – adults are usually a mottled, olive-green colour with yellow and black lines running down either side of their body.

Quite a few had lost tails, while one or two appeared to have regenerated theirs. We started to count how many we were seeing, and by the time we got to the hide, had reached 22, though a girl who was staying at the nearby caravan park had apparently surpassed 50 only the day before – still, it was easily the highest number of lizards I'd ever seen in Britain in one place in the space of the 15 minutes or so.

39 RING-NECKED PARAKEETS

KENSINGTON GARDENS

Family friendly ★★★★★
Parrots that will feed out of your hand

Budget friendly ★★★★★
It's a public park in Central London

Amateur friendly ★★★★
Hard to mistake parakeets for anything else

Best time of year
All year round

Toilets ✓
Cafe ✓

© James Fair

Is there a more unlikely location for a great wildlife experience than Kensington Gardens in Central London? Not in my book!

To the purist, ring-necked parakeets, like grey squirrels, are an alien species, but to others, they're now an established part of our fauna (again, like grey squirrels), and there's no getting rid of them. They're all over the South-east of England – I've seen them at my sister's allotment in Raynes Park, during a gig in Chelsea and in Knole Park in Sevenoaks in Kent.

DO IT YOURSELF

Kensington Gardens is in the heart of Central London and separated from Hyde Park by West Carriage Drive. Paddington is the nearest mainline train station about a 10-minute walk away.

Walk south from the Italian Gardens at the top of The Long Water (which turns into the Serpentine in Hyde Park) and then past the Peter Pan statue, and you'll find the parakeets. They seem to like nuts best, but take unsalted ones, and don't hand out too many. Kensington Gardens ⌕ www.royalparks.org.uk/parks/kensington-gardens ☎ 0300 061 2000

Like most parrots, they're a species of the tropics, found in Central Africa and much of the Indian subcontinent. But, they escaped, or were deliberately released, from aviaries in Britain in the 1970s, and have since done rather well here. Some reports suggest there are up to 50,000 of them in the South-east today.

Like other parrots, they're intelligent, sociable birds that quickly lose their fear of humans. In Kensington Gardens, the best place to go is just south of the Italian Gardens, on the west side of the Serpentine just after the Peter Pan statue. If it sounds complicated, when I visited they were impossible to miss.

They were perched low on trees and bushes looking beadily around as if waiting for the next meal, and they immediately perked up as I put down my rucksack and opened a packet of dried fruit and nuts.

I put some in my hand and waited. One or two started to sidle closer, using their beaks as an extra limb as they worked their way down the branches. Eventually, one bold individual flew down, then changed its mind at the last minute and returned to the perch. But within a minute or two, it had landed on my hand and was tucking into the nuts.

Then a funny thing happened. I decided it had had enough free food for the day and put the packet away, at which point I expected the parakeet to leave me alone. Instead, it hopped onto my jacket sleeve as if we were now friends. When I gently tried to shoo it away, it hopped onto my shoulder. It felt as if I could have walked out of the park and down Pall Mall, and it wouldn't have moved.

38 PLUNGE-DIVING TERNS

COQUET ISLAND, NORTHUMBERLAND

Family friendly ★★★★
A short boat ride on a former lifeboat to watch seals, as well as thousands of terns

Budget friendly ★★★
Will cost about £20 for a family of four

Amateur friendly ★★★★
If you're not bothered about telling your Arctic, common, roseate and sandwich terns apart, yes

Best time of year
May-August

Toilets (in Amble) ✓
Cafe (in Amble) ✓

As the iconic RNLI orange-and-blue livery hove into view where we stood on the Amble quayside, it struck me that I wouldn't necessarily want to see this battered old boat coming to save me in a crisis. But I trusted it to take us the few miles out to Coquet Island and back, and besides it was an old lifeboat – the children were happy.

DO IT YOURSELF

Only one operator takes tourists around Coquet Island – Dave Gray's Puffin Cruises. It has two boats, the *G Fisher* and the former lifeboat *RNLB Beryl Tollemache*. ☌ www.puffincruises. co.uk ☎ 07752 861914 or 01665 711975. I recommend calling until someone answers, because they didn't return calls or respond to emails, but on the other hand, booking didn't seem to be necessary.

Directions in Amble aren't very clear, but we ended up in the car park on Harbour Road. From there, the boats leave from the obvious small dock less than a five-minute walk due west.

More information about Coquet Island from the RSPB. ☌ www.rspb.org/coquetisland ☎ 0300 7772 676

Among birders, Coquet is renowned as a breeding site for the seriously rare (in Britain and indeed Europe, anyway) roseate tern – just over 100 pairs breed here, by far our most significant colony. Like many terns, they have dagger-like beaks, smart glossy white breasts, black caps and long tail feathers or streamers, though the roseate gets its name from the pinkish hue they acquire during the breeding season.

But if you are, as I was, clutching a small child who's suddenly started to panic at the prospect of going out to sea (even a just a mile or so) on a boat that's bobbing up and down on a choppy sea, it's unsurprisingly hard to concentrate on the pinkish hue to a bird's breast or its longer-than-usual tail streamers.

The geek inside me was annoyed at first, but it really didn't matter – there were hundreds of terns plunge-diving all around us, and though they're tiny compared with gannets (**Experience 7**), that's part of the spectacle of these delicate, determined and oddly furious little seabirds. They were a constant barrage of activity, hovering no more than a few metres above the water, then – Zip! – down where they catch sandeels from the surface.

There are some 35,000 seabirds nesting on Coquet in the summer months, and it feels on a trip around the island – you can't land – that about half of those are fishing for their tea at any one time. In any direction you look, there's a tiny, terrifying projectile flying furiously into the waves. It's a sight truly to gladden the heart.

37 SNAKE'S-HEAD FRITILLARIES

UPPER WATERHAY AND NORTH MEADOW

Family friendly ★★★
Kids are not, in my experience, especially wowed by flowers, but at worst, this is a pleasant, easy walk

Budget friendly ★★★★★
The reserve is free

Amateur friendly ★★★★
As long as you can find your way there – getting to Upper Waterhay requires (fairly modest) navigation skills

Best time of year
Just two short weeks in mid-April

As I approached the Wiltshire Wildlife Trust reserve of Upper Waterhay, just outside the town of Cricklade, I wasn't sure what to expect. All I knew was that it was a small field of wildflowers called snake's-head fritillaries, but that it was unusual because the majority of them were white as opposed to the more standard dark purple of their blooms.

Then, unexpectedly, I caught a glimpse of it. From a distance, the whole field was thickly covered in white flowers giving the appearance of a lush

---

DO IT YOURSELF

Upper Waterhay is just outside the town of Cricklade. From the village of Ashton Keynes, head east as if going to Cricklade. There's an obvious car park after 1km, just before the road crosses the river. Park here and carry on along the road for just over 0.5km – between Brook and Manor Farms, there is a track on the left. Upper Waterhay is another 200m down here. An OS map is helpful for finding it. ⌖ www.wiltshirewildlife.org/upper-waterhay-cricklade ☎ 01380 725670

North Meadow is just north of Cricklade – leave the town as if heading back to the A419, and it's on your left. There's a sign marking the main entrance. ⌖ crickladeinbloom.co.uk/fritillary_watch.html ☎ 01452 813982

white-green carpet that was quite unlike anything I'd ever seen before. Entering the field, I realised it was an illusion, but still in an area the size of perhaps two or three football pitches, there were thousands upon thousands of these delicate, drooping beauties.

And in some ways, this is the less spectacular experience. The nearby North Meadow is a billiard-table flat expanse of floodplain that is said to be home to 1.5 million snake's-head fritillaries.

It's an experience that creeps up on you. On entering the meadow, you may not see much more than a huge field of short-cropped grass. Here and there, you might just make out a faint purple haze. Start walking around the field in an anti-clockwise direction, and before long you will start to realise that the haze you've already spotted is clusters of hundreds, if not thousands and tens of thousands of flowers their slightly outsized bulbous heads hanging down like lanterns.

Crouch or even lie down – making sure you aren't crushing any plants in the process – and look at them close up, and you'll notice the snake-skin pattern from which you'd think they get their name – in fact, it's the shape of the flower bud that resembles a snake about to strike. Most of them are purple, but about one in 10 are the same creamy white as those at Upper Waterhay.

36 BADGER WATCHING

NANNERTH FARM, RHAYADER

Family friendly ★★★

Yes – but wannabe badger-
watchers need to be quiet and
stay up until after it's dark

Budget friendly ★★★★

Nannerth Farm is holiday
accommodation with a unique
badger 'hide', but you can
also arrange to go with your
local badger group for next to
nothing

Amateur friendly ★★★★★

One of our most easily
recognised mammals

Best time of year

April-Oct

© James Fair

Many dairy and beef cattle farmers notwithstanding, there's little doubt that the badger is one of Britain's favourite wild animals – in a poll carried out

---

DO IT YOURSELF

Nannerth Farm (LD6 5HA) has a hide built into an oak tree for a unique badger-watching experience. It has room for six people, and children are welcome, but noise will deter the badgers. The farm has a range of self-catering accommodation, but the hide can be booked by people not staying there. ⚘ www.nannerth.co.uk ☎ 01597 811121

The Badger Trust has a network of local groups, many of which will run badger-watching evenings. Find your local county group through its website. ⚘ www.badger.org.uk/local-groups ☎ 0845 8287878

Alternatively, if you think your garden is anywhere near a badger sett, or there's a clear sign that something's been digging up your lawn, put out peanuts to see if you can watch them from your back door.

by *BBC Wildlife Magazine*, to find a national wildlife icon, it came second to the hedgehog. But while encounters with hedgehogs cannot usually be arranged, badgers are more predictable creatures, and – with a casual scattering of peanuts – relatively easy to tempt into places where they can be watched.

With the absence of our top native predators (bears, wolves and lynx), they are now our largest terrestrial carnivores, but despite an armoury of powerful jaws and long, raking claws, they eat mainly earthworms (80 per cent of their diet), so their search for food is nothing more menacing than bumbling along a favoured pasture with snouts close to the ground, sniffing out dinner with their powerful sense of smell.

Perhaps this is why they hold a special place in the nation's collective heart – that and the uniquely black-and-white striped head and salt-and-pepper fur which mean it's impossible to mistake a badger for anything else.

Not everyone feels well-disposed towards badgers. The British government began a controversial cull in 2013 in an attempt to reduce levels of bovine tuberculosis (bTB) in cattle, and this cull has since been rolled out to everywhere from Cornwall to Cumbria. It is controversial for two main reasons: first, because badgers are fully protected, and second because most scientists either say badgers aren't the problem or a cull won't work.

Some home-owners can also harbour anti-badger emotions when they see the damage inflicted on a well-tended lawn – clods of turf ripped up (those raking claws have a serious purpose), the bowling-green surface degraded by forces beyond their horticultural control. Our lawn, too, suffers this treatment on a regular basis, but I prefer to see it in a positive light, a sense of the wild even on our suburban doorstep.

35 HOVERING KESTRELS

Family friendly ★★★
Something intangibly exciting about a hunting kestrel

Budget friendly ★★★★★
There's no need to pay to see a kestrel

Amateur friendly ★★★
Some skills needed in knowing where to look, but they are very distinctive

Best time of year
All year round, but they won't hunt much on very wet or windy days

I remember first becoming aware of kestrels while going on holiday as a child. Driving down the M3 and then along the A303 on our way to Devon, we'd regularly see kestrels hovering by the side of the road as they hunted for field or bank voles in the grassy verges. It always seemed an unlikely setting for such a fabulous, exciting bird. I don't think we actually referred to it as the 'motorway bird', but that was how I thought of it.

It's my impression that you don't see them so often alongside major roads these days, and certainly their numbers have declined in the past 30 or 40 years. There may be other reasons why you see them less frequently roadsides, however – in some parts of Britain, red kites (**Experience 16**) have returned in huge numbers thanks to reintroduction programmes, and they love to monitor motorways such as the M42 and M4 for roadkill. So perhaps kestrels, which are considerably smaller than red kites, have been ousted from these hunting spots in some areas.

I always keep my eyes peeled for them, nonetheless. 'Keep your eyes on

DO IT YOURSELF

There is no surefire way of finding a kestrel. As already stated in the main text, they are frequently (but less frequently than 30 years ago) seen alongside motorways and other main roads, but any areas of open grassland or scrub potentially provides habitat for them. They are slightly more widespread in central and eastern England than in Wales, the South-west or Scotland.

the road!' screams my partner as I'm trying to point out the hovering bird to my kids in the back of the car, who in turn wail, 'Where? Where? I can't see it!' She has a point, but there really is nothing like watching these small, delicate birds of prey, their wings beating rapidly to keep themselves stock still and their eyes fixed on the ground.

Unfortunately, there's no way of guaranteeing an encounter with a kestrel – like foxes or otters, sightings are mostly random. But there are a few tips that are worth remembering – they're birds of open fields or moorland, and can be seen right across Britain, including on the coast (in some areas, this can be excellent habitat for them). The only places you definitely won't see them are properly urban areas (but you might in city or town parks), thick forest or woodland and high mountains.

You often first notice them as they pull out of a hover, and it's that russet-coloured back and those black wingtips that stand out and couldn't belong to any other bird here in the UK. If you're lucky, you'll watch them as they fall, or stoop, but remember, if you're driving – 'Keep your eyes on the road!'

34 CALLING GREENSHANKS

FORSINARD FLOWS RSPB RESERVE, CAITHNESS & SUTHERLAND

Family friendly ★★★
Worth going for the train ride alone

Budget friendly ★★★★
A very remote location, but free once you get there

Amateur friendly ★★
A very hard bird to spot during the breeding season – the call is distinctive, however

Best time of year
April-June

Toilets ✓

If the so-called Flow Country in north-east Scotland isn't the strangest landscape in mainland Britain, I don't know what is. There are huge tracts of pancake-flat bog that remind me of the interior of Estonia (though admittedly I've only ever seen it in photos), and on my only visit to 'the Flows', I half expected to see a moose – or elk, as we call them in Europe – lumbering through the swamp and to be eaten alive by mosquitoes. (I didn't and I wasn't.)

There are few roads, though there is handy railway line with a stop at Forsinard, and tumbling out of the tiny shuttle train at the deserted station reminded me of a scene from a Western. No tumbleweed, as such, but it felt as if there should have been. The train ride is an adventure in itself, the line crisscrossing the river where wader-clad fly fishermen were trying their luck in water the colour of cold tea.

DO IT YOURSELF

RSPB Forsinard Flows (KW13 6YT) is truly in the back of beyond – the nearest big town is probably Thurso, almost 50km to the north-east. Forsinard station gives you very easy access to the tower and is on the line between Inverness and Thurso/Wick. ⌨ www.rspb.org.uk/forsinard ☎ 01641 571225

The RSPB has recently installed a boardwalk that goes out over the peatbog (you'd probably sink up to your knees without it), and this leads to a surreal-looking, one-storey tower offering views over the wider area. I climbed the tower, expecting to hear the sound of a burbling curlew or trilling skylark, but there was an eerie, deathly silence. Even the wind made little noise – there were no trees to rustle, no branches to sway.

Then I heard something I didn't recognise – an insistent, two-tone call, some distance away, that resembled a rather frantic car alarm. It came in bursts of 5 or 10 seconds, fell silent then started up again. It wasn't beautiful, but its oddness matched the landscape. The call was unknown to me, but it didn't take me long to track down the culprit by listening to recordings of possible suspects (it had to be a wader, I deduced) – it was a greenshank, a small wader with – as you'd expect – dark green legs.

And, in hindsight, it turns out I wasn't wrong to imagine an air of mystery about this bird. By all accounts, its nests are the hardest to find of any British breeding bird, almost impossible to detect unless you are very lucky. But I didn't need to see either a nest or the bird itself – the call, carrying through the still evening air and over the dark, peaty lochans, was enough to satisfy my craving for wilderness in this enigmatic country.

33 FOSSIL-HUNTING

CHARMOUTH

Family friendly ★★★★★
A brilliant activity to do with children

Budget friendly ★★★★
Guided fossil walks are great value for money – £8 for adults, £4 for children

Amateur friendly ★★
You stand a much better chance of finding and identifying fossils if you go on a guided walk

Best time of year
All year round

Toilets ✓
Cafe ✓

© James Fair.

Fossils aren't, strictly speaking, wildlife, but they were once, and the childish excitement you experience from unearthing something that lived and breathed hundreds of millions of years ago is hard to beat. And, there's few better places in Britain to go on a Jurassic hunt than Charmouth.

DO IT YOURSELF

Fossil walks can be booked through Charmouth Heritage Coast Centre (DT6 6LL). ⌂ charmouth.org/chcc ☎ 01297 560772

If you want to fossil-hunt on your own, head west (right) from the main centre at Charmouth until you reach an area of small medium sized stones and boulders lying on gravelly sand. The fossils are best found in this sand – just sift through it with your fingers.

There are plenty of other locations in Britain to go fossil hunting, though Dorset's Jurassic coast is without question the best in the country. Try UK Fossils Network for ideas. ⌂ ukfossils.co.uk

And while you're never going to dig up the complete skeleton of a *T. Rex* – they were running around North America millions of years after the animals found here were alive – there is a reasonable chance of unearthing a bone belonging to a *Scelidosaurus*, dumpy marsh-loving dinosaurs that have only ever been found in this part of Dorset.

But if the more mundane fare of ammonites and belemnites (tiny, bullet-shaped fossils that are the internal skeletons of ancient squid) is spiced up with the occasional *Scelidosaurus* vertebra, then you'll have done well, and anything you find is yours to keep.

My nine-year-old son, Sam, took to scrabbling among the beach boulders with great gusto, and we were particularly pleased with the ammonites that had been fossilised with iron pyrites – tiny but perfectly formed, with just a hint of the shininess that gives pyrites the alternative name of fool's gold. The calcite ammonite was another good find with its shiny, marble-like surface.

Sam was particularly adept at unearthing belemnites, though we got nowhere near the figure of 562 that our fossil guide said was the record for a group on one of their walks. 'One time, we spotted someone throwing away something that turned out to be the thigh bone of a *Scelidosaurus*,' she said with glee in an excellent pre-hunt pep talk that was both accessible for six-year-olds and entertaining and useful for adults.

The other thing to realise about Charmouth is that it is a truly sustainable resource – the entire cliff face is being constantly eroded by the power of the sea and other forces, spewing up new specimens on a regular basis.

As it neared the end of the day, Sam was still sifting away, desperate to get his hands on a *Scelidosaurus* vertebra. We'll be back.

32 SOARING FULMARS

NOUP CLIFFS RSPB RESERVE, WESTRAY

Family friendly ★★★
Though Noup Cliffs is very remote, you can drive right up to the Noup Head Lighthouse (on a fairly rough track)

Budget friendly ★★★
No cost apart from getting to Orkney

Amateur friendly ★★★★
Fulmars are distinctive seabirds – learn to distinguish them from gulls

Best time of year
March-Oct (though fulmars can be seen for most of the year)

Though the occasional vagrant – otherwise known as lost – albatross turns up off the coast of Britain from time to time, on the whole they are a group of spectacular birds that confine themselves to the Southern Hemisphere.

This is a shame – I'd loved to have been able to include 'black-browed albatross' in my 100 list of things to see in the UK, but you'd need to spend several weeks of your life staring out to sea in probably gale-force winds at Flamborough Head, on the coast of East Yorkshire, to give yourself even a small chance of ticking that particular beauty. Probably easier and warmer just to go to South Georgia, really.

DO IT YOURSELF

Noup Cliffs RSPB Reserve is a spectacular cliff-top reserve on the island of Westray, north-east of Orkney Mainland. It has a sizeable gannet colony, along with great skuas and fulmars. ☞ www.rspb.org/noupcliffs ☎ 01856 850176

There are plenty of other locations both in mainland Britain and on islands to see fulmars – from the Isles of Scilly in the English Channel, to Skomer Island off Wales, Flamborough Head in East Yorkshire, they really are very widespread.

So, instead I'll go with the next best thing – the easy-to-see fulmar, a seabird that may superficially resemble your average gull but is actually quite distinct. It is part of a large group of birds that also includes albatrosses and which are linked by similar structures within their beaks – you can see this 'tubenose' on fulmars as a small appendage on top of their beaks. They can excrete a foul-smelling, oily substance which (it is said) can ruin your clothes. So beware.

They also have a very distinctive flight (and this also links them to albatrosses), soaring – especially in strong winds – on very stiff wings. Watching fulmars riding the winds along a cliff edge or performing wide, lazy figures of eight above a bay, seemingly for no other purpose than because they can, is something I can enjoy again and again. Indeed, they may be doing it purely because they can – the travel writer and naturalist Adam Nicolson reports in his book *The Seabird's Cry* that scientists have found, in winds above 20mph, fulmars expend the same amount of energy gliding as they do sitting on a nest.

At Noup, you can also watch them on their nests, the chicks all fluffy and grey and often left alone for long periods, but they are common throughout much of Britain, so it's always worth keeping an eye out for their characteristic and charismatic flight.

31 DAWN EXODUS

HAM WALL RSPB RESERVE, ASHCOTT

Family friendly ★

Early start, cold mornings = no children

Budget friendly ★★★★

Just the carpark to pay for, unless you're an RSPB member

Amateur friendly ★★★★

On the whole yes – it would be good if you swotted up on some of your water-bird ID skills

Best time of year

Dec-Feb

Toilets ✓
Café (basic hot drinks, not much else) ✓

It started with a low thrum. I turned round and hundreds of starlings were flying towards me in a great mass, hurrying onwards in a Gadarene rush. They were just 10 or 20 feet above my head and stayed low, dipping down towards the lake and its reedbed then lifting up over it and away into the gloom.

I looked up, and over on the far side of the lake, there was a stream of thousands, perhaps tens of thousands, of birds also leaving their night roost, staying close together to form a dense black cloud. The starlings had spent

DO IT YOURSELF

Ham Wall RSPB Reserve (BA6 9SX) says it may be worth calling the 'starling hotline' (07866 554142) to find out where they roosted the previous evening. ⌂ www.rspb.org/hamwall ☎ 01458 860494

Other good wetlands may provide similar experiences. Try Leighton Moss (LA5 0SW, Experience 9), Minsmere (IP17 3BY, Experience 44) or Saltholme RSPB Reserve (TS2 1TP, ⌂ www.rspb.org/saltholme ☎ 01642 546625).

the night roosting in the reedbed, and now they were pouring from their sleeping posts like insects that had been trapped in a jar, and in less than 20-30 minutes, they were all gone. It was fun, but nothing compared to a really exhilarating evening murmuration (**Experience 11**).

But on the other side of the track – an old railway line that runs the length of Ham Wall, providing neat access (with the helpline of branchline boardwalks) to the reserve's various nooks and crannies – other birds began to stir. There had been occasional calls and whistles from the coots, tufted ducks, wigeons and shelducks that had spent the night there, but then a flock of lapwings unexpectedly took to the sky.

There must have been several hundred in the group, and it flew high over the lake, sometimes clustered so close it nearly took on the shape-shifting qualities of a starling murmuration. It wheeled round in an arc, some of the outliers passing in front of the waning moon, over the track then back again, with none of the manic purpose of the starlings.

From time to time, they settled back down in the shallow areas of the lake, forming neat rows, staring dull-eyed into the middle distance – but then they'd be off again, for no reason that I could determine. At one point, I saw a sparrowhawk being mobbed by crows, then a buzzard sitting impassively on a distant tree, but neither of these greatly threatened the lapwings. The whole display lasted half an hour or more, and defiantly outperformed the starling dawn exodus I had come to see.

30 SWIMMING WITH PUFFINS

SKOMER, PEMBROKESHIRE

Family friendly ★★
Difficult for young children –
possible for teenagers who are
competent swimmers

Budget friendly ★★
Puffins tend to live in remote
locations

Amateur friendly ★★★★
At least anyone can recognise
a puffin

Best time of year
May-August (but the sea is still
very cold in May!)

© www.andydavies.info.

Before taking the plunge, I did a quick check of my equipment – mask and snorkel, tick; fins, tick; decoy puffin and lanyard, tick. Decoy puffin? Well, how else are you going to get the puffins to come close to you?

I was in South Haven, on the island of Skomer, with wildlife guide and photographer Andy Davies, who was supposed to be teaching me how to photograph puffins under water. After trying to swim and take pictures

---

DO IT YOURSELF

This is sadly very hard to do for yourself. Wildlife guide Andy Davies doesn't currently run puffin photography workshops on Skomer, but that could change. ☝ www.andydavies. info ☎ 01269 871870

There's one other place I know where you could conceivably swim with puffins – the Shiant Isles (Experience 51), in the Outer Hebrides. It's very remote, and few commercial operators run trips out there. More information on the Shiant Isles website. www.shiantisles.net

Sea Harris runs private charter trips out there. ☝ seaharris.com/the-trip/private-charters/ shiants ☎ 01859 502007. Northern Light Cruising will also stop there. ☝ www.northernlight-uk.com/islands/the-shiant-islands ☎ 01599 555723

---

at the same time (not my forte), I ended up crouching on a rock that was submerged a few feet below the surface, thrusting the decoy out in front of me and waiting. It didn't take long. Puffins are curious creatures, and they were keen to investigate. I took a few pictures at the surface, then tried and failed to get some shots with a split-level view (half-above and half-below the water).

But it was when I dived down myself, giving up all pretensions of photography, that I saw them for what they really are. All around me, there were puffins fizzing through the water, and freed from terrestrial constraints, they were transformed from clumsy clowns, or the clockwork toys they resemble in flight, to lithe and graceful predators. They looked so at home down there, using their wings as flippers to speed through the water, small streams of bubbles showing a tiny trace of where they'd been. Who's the clumsy one, now, I thought?

In this respect, they reminded me of penguins, which is less surprising than it sounds – the auk family, to which puffins belong, are the Northern Hemisphere's equivalent of penguins. One, called the great auk, was the size of a king penguin and likewise couldn't fly. Indeed, the great auk was called penguin before penguins were – when European explorers reached Antarctica they named the birds they found after those they resembled from back home.

Sadly, the great auk – much like the dodo – was full of tasty meat, covered in lovely feathers that could be used as down and was easy to kill; the world's last confirmed pair were killed off Iceland in 1844. Let's hope puffins can be saved from their relative's fate.

29 GLOW WORMS

WESTBURY-SUB-MENDIP

Family friendly ★★★★
Insects glowing an atomic green has got to be a hit with children

Budget friendly ★★★★★
Guided walks are very cheap

Amateur friendly ★★★
Even though they glow, they may be hard to find on your own

Best time of year
July and August

Two middle-aged men wandering down a quiet country lane and staring intently into the hedgerows on either side, saying things such as, 'Nope, must have imagined it,' could easily be misinterpreted. So it's probably a good thing that the only other people we saw that evening were doing the same as us. Indeed, the boy, who looked about 11, had seen

DO IT YOURSELF

Westbury-sub-Mendip is a village in Somerset just north-west of Wells. Park at the recreation ground on Roughmoor Lane, then walk down Roughmoor Lane (heading west). Start out just as it is getting properly dark.

Somerset Wildlife Trust organises guided walks in Westbury-sub-Mendip with local expert Peter Bright. ⌁ www.somersetwildlife.org ☎ 01823 652400

Glow worms emerge for mating between June and September, but July and August are the best months to see them.

The Great Orme, in North Wales, is reputedly one of the places in Britain to see glow worms. You can find out if there are any glow worm guided walks in your area on this website: ⌁ www.glowworms.org.uk/#Glow_worm_evenings

36 the previous week. We might need his expertise, I thought, but as it turned out, we didn't.

Glow worms are not worms, they're Britain's only species of firefly, a group of insects better known for their fabulous light displays in South-east Asia. And fireflies, just to be clear, aren't flies – they're beetles. So, badly named all round, but that doesn't detract from the experience.

It's the female that glows, illuminating her abdomen, in a bright-green, citrusy hue that looks so good you could eat it, in order to attract a male. But, at the same time, she doesn't want to attract unwanted attention, so she only turns herself on (as it were) once hidden away in a hedgerow – hence the reason for our hard stares. It was surprising how often I mistook what was left of the daylight reflecting off a leaf or twig for our quarry.

Perhaps it just takes a while to get your eye in, but certainly by the time night had properly fallen and we'd been out for an hour, we were seeing glow worms in the hedge every ten yards. For many of them, you have to do what we christened the glow-worm shuffle, which involves ducking and twisting your head in order to have exactly the right line of sight into the hedge.

And what a sight – this bright, almost nuclear, green body, sitting there patiently in the darkness, waiting for her man. A final stroll around Westbury's 'rec' brought our total for the evening to 41, one short of the answer to life, the universe and everything. That seemed about right.

28 BEAVERS

OTTERTON

Family friendly ★★★
A short, easy walk, but if you want to see the beavers, you'll need to be quiet and patient

Budget friendly ★★★★★
This one's free

Amateur friendly ★★★
Beavers are shy and may be hard to spot

Best time of year
May-Sept

Toilets ✓
Cafe ✓

© Mike Symes/Devon Wildlife Trust.

With its white-washed houses and thatched roofs, the village of Otterton in East Devon makes you feel like you're taking a gentle trip back a few decades

DO IT YOURSELF

Follow the footpath, clearly marked on the OS map, which tracks the River Otter north from Otterton. You pass a weir after about five minutes, then an elegant wooden bridge after another five. The footpath veers away from the river slightly, and where it comes back is the beaver's lodge.

Beavers are mainly nocturnal. Your best chance of seeing them is during the spring and summer (May-Sept), when days are longest, and they are out while it is still light. Go an hour or so before dusk or at very first light in the morning.

Devon Wildlife Trust monitors the beavers and will have the most up-to-date information on where to find them. ᕗ www.devonwildlifetrust.org ☎ 01392 279244

You can also visit Knapdale, on Scotland's west coast, to see their beavers. www.scottishbeavers.org.uk/visit-knapdale

in time. But take a dawn or dusk stroll along the River Otter, and you can go back centuries.

The river – which flows into the sea at Budleigh Salterton – is home to England's only recognised wild beavers. Native to Britain until they were hunted to extinction in the sixteenth century, beavers are slowly making a comeback, first in Scotland and now south of the border, thanks to one official reintroduction project and some unsanctioned releases. On the River Otter, there are said to be five family groups, though the population is quite dynamic and growing fast.

With my partner and two children, at first light one morning in early August, we walked for about a mile on the footpath that runs north along the River Otter from Otterton. There was no trouble finding the spot where one of the females had her home because there were three other eager beaver watchers, their eyes trained intently on a mass of green foliage on the other side of the river, which turned out to be the beaver's lodge.

A woman, who had come all the way from Essex to see them, showed us footage she'd taken only moments earlier of the female grooming one of her kits – if only, my partner sighed, she hadn't had that cup of tea. Then there was a splash, and suddenly, incredibly, we were watching the same female swimming towards her lodge. A quick flick of the tail, and she was gone, diving to reach her home through its underwater entrance. That was my first-ever sighting of a beaver of any description – let alone a wild one, let alone here in England.

Science shows that the way in which beavers re-engineer their habitat by damming rivers and felling trees provides environmental benefits by holding back the flow to reduce downstream flooding, while also filtering out pollutants. There may be more beaver reintroductions in Britain in the near future, in which case a visit to Otterton will be like going back to the future, as well the past.

27 BOTTLENOSE DOLPHINS

NEW QUAY, CARDIGAN BAY

Family friendly ★★★★★
Perfect for children

Budget friendly ★★
Expect to pay £50-60 for a family of four for a 1½-2 hour trip

Amateur friendly ★★★★★
Boats have on board guides who know how to spot the dolphins

Best time of year
April-Sept

© Peter Evans/Sea Watch Foundation

Standing on the causeway that forms the harbour in New Quay, I was staring out into Cardigan Bay in the hopeful way I do when I'm by the seaside. The people around us were relaxing on deckchairs or scoffing ice creams, so no one else noticed the gun-metal grey dorsal fin breaking the surface of the water some distance away. We were taking a boat trip in half an hour, but here in New Quay, the dolphins come to you, it seemed.

DO IT YOURSELF

A number of operators offer trips to see the dolphins. I'd recommend those run by New Quay Boat Trips, because they have trained volunteers on their boats and data obtained on these trips is used to help conservation of the dolphins. ☌ www.newquayboattrips.co.uk ☎ 01545 560800

Other operators include Cardigan Bay Marine Wildlife Centre (☌ www.welshwildlife.org/visitor-centres/cardigan-bay-marine-wildlife-centre ☎ 01545 560032) and SeaMor (☌ www.seamor.org ☎ 07795 242445).

The Sea Watch Foundation is a very useful source of information about marine wildlife and wants to hear about your whale and dolphin sightings. ☌ www.seawatchfoundation.org.uk ☎ 01545 561227

There are only really four places off Britain where you can reliably see bottlenose dolphins, uniformly grey, large cetaceans sporting that permanent (misleading) smile. The first is in the Moray Firth, on Scotland's east coast – there's even a well-known spot called Chanonry Point where you can stand on the foreshore and watch dolphins feeding on the incoming tide less than 50 metres away.

The second is the Hebrides, but this is less good because it's such a large area, and sightings are far from guaranteed. Whale-watching boats leave from Tobermory on Mull most days in the spring and summer. The third is off Cornwall, where scientists have only just recognised there is a resident group.

The fourth location – Cardigan Bay – is the best in my view, mainly because sightings are so reliable, but partly because it seems so unlikely as you head down through the town passing shops selling gaudy buckets and spades, wind-breakers and fish and chips.

After spotting our single dolphin in the bay, we were soon heading south along the coast, passing small colonies of guillemots and razorbills, and it wasn't long before the dolphins themselves appeared. It was a small group of about six or seven individuals, and they were feeding, their glistening grey bodies surfacing every couple of minutes. There was one with a calf, always in perfect harmony with its mother.

There was one time when I watched hundreds of bottlenose dolphins engage in a spectacular breaching display. At one point, two dolphins leapt simultaneously from the water, crossed in mid-air and re-entered the water in perfect symmetry. But I'm cheating – that was in Tasmania. It was exactly the same species as our bottlenose dolphin, though, so it just shows what they can do if the mood takes them.

© Peter Evans/Sea Watch Foundation

26 BUGLING CRANES

ALLER MOOR, NEAR LANGPORT

Family friendly ★
No – leave the kids behind.
The levels can be terrifyingly
cold in mid-winter, and you're
unlikely to get very close to the
cranes

Budget friendly ★★★★★
Nothing to pay, unless you go
on a guided walk

Amateur friendly ★
Despite their size, they are
remarkably hard to spot

Best time of year
Dec-Feb

Eight birds took off from the field, looking – with their small heads, long graceful necks, slim bodies and black-tipped wings that appeared from a distance to be pointed – like avian versions of Concorde. They slowly gained height, and wheeled round before heading behind some

DO IT YOURSELF

Aller Moor and West Sedgemoor, in the southern section of the Somerset Levels, have become the favoured winter feeding and roosting grounds for the reintroduced cranes.

Try looking for them from the River Parrett Trail (clearly marked on the Ordnance Survey map) that runs between Langport and Burrowbridge. The Great Crane Project (the partnership of conservation organisations that reintroduced the canes into the levels) recommends the section between Oath Lock and Stathe, looking out over Aller Moor to the north-east. Arrive at first light, because they will be hungry and feeding. ✎ www.thegreatcraneproject.org.uk – there's no phone number, but you can contact the project via the website.

West Sedgemoor RSPB Reserve (TA10 0PH) runs guided walks, and the cranes can also be seen there. ✎ www.rspb.org/westsedgemoor ☎ 01458 252805

tall trees some 400 metres away. Their collective mind seemed unsure what to do next, but eventually they came down, out of sight, on the far side of those trees. It was a brief but exhilarating view of a species that disappeared from this landscape for the best part of 500 years.

Cranes went extinct in Britain at the end of the sixteenth century but re-established naturally in the Norfolk Broads in the late 1970s. They remained absent from the west of Britain until a number of conservation organisations banded together to reintroduce them into the Somerset Levels in 2009 – helping to secure their future in the UK.

Cranes are birds of lowland moors and bogs, requiring large areas of low-intensity farmed land to thrive, and hearing their bugling calls, which carried over long distances on the flat and mainly treeless terrain, gave me goosebumps, a real feeling of wildness that it's hard to encounter in most of England today.

They are big birds, too, standing up to 1.3 metres and high and with a wingspan of more than 2 metres. As of late 2017, there are an estimated 55 cranes in the levels. During the summer, they disperse to pair up and breed and are extremely hard to see, but in the winter, they congregate in larger groups, often around Aller Moor, to the north-west of Langport, and are easier to locate.

Towards the end of winter, there is another reason for going in search of them – come early February, pairs begin the elaborate courtship displays that will hopefully end in them rearing chicks.

25 SWALLOWTAIL BUTTERFLIES

STRUMPSHAW FEN RSPB RESERVE

Family friendly ★★★★
Easy to find, large butterflies –
great for kids

Budget friendly ★★★★
Entry to the reserve is free
to RSPB members – non-
members are charged £3.50 for
adults, £1.50 for children

Amateur friendly ★★★★
Swallowtail butterflies are very
distinctive

Best time of year
June

Toilets ✓
Cafe ✓

For such beautiful animals, swallowtail butterflies have a bit of a sordid past. They start life as tiny orange-yellow eggs laid on milk parsley – a fussy plant that only grows in a few parts of Britain – and these hatch into small black caterpillars. One female swallowtail lays a single egg on a single plant, but – in lean years for milk parsley – other females will come along and lay their eggs there too.

As the larvae develop, growing green and fat, they start to exhaust the resources of the milk parsley on which they have so far been nourished, and they turn their attention on each other – as in *The Hunger Games*, they must now fight, kill and eat (so that bit goes a bit beyond the film's storyline) each other until there is only one left on the mother plant. Once the sole remaining caterpillar is fully grown, it spins itself a pupa where it will ride out the next nine months until springtime of the following year.

Swallowtails are confined to Norfolk in this country (they are very common in mainland Europe) because milk parsley only grows in the warm and wet conditions of the fens (which are essentially marshland areas typical of East Anglia and with neutral or alkaline water chemistry).

On my trip to Strumpshaw, it wasn't long before we'd found one, sipping nectar from the spectacular yellow flag irises that are also common there. And what a glory this beast was – with a wingspan as big as a child's hand and those exotic 'tails' on the undersides of its lower wings, it looked as though had just flown in from St Tropez. The signature yellow and blue colouration, that makes the species so unmistakable, is said to be even more vibrant on the butterflies that are found here compared to elsewhere.

24 OSPREY ACTION

LOCH GARTEN RSPB RESERVE, CAIRNGORMS NP

Family friendly ★★★★
Easy, almost guaranteed
sightings of this fish-eating
raptor

Budget friendly ★★★★
Free to RSPB members – a
family of four non-members
would pay £10

Amateur friendly ★★★★★
Easy to spot the ospreys, and
expert RSPB staff on hand to
help out too

Best time of year
April-Sept

Toilets ✓

The female osprey was having none of it. The crow was probably hanging around in case it could pinch an egg or two, the RSPB's Chris Tilbury told me, so an amazing dogfight ensued, with the much larger bird of prey snapping at the heels of the wily, agile corvid. In general, the female sits tight on the nest and lets the

---

DO IT YOURSELF

Loch Garten RSPB Reserve (PH25 3EF) is part of Abernethy National Nature Reserve in the north-west of Cairngorms NP, about a 20-minute drive outside of Aviemore. ᗣ www.rspb.org/lochgarten ☎ 01479 831476

Dornoch Firth, together with Loch Fleet National Nature Reserve, has special protection because of its breeding ospreys. ᗣ www.nnr.scot/Search_by_AZ ☎ 0300 067 6841

Other good places for ospreys include Bassenthwaite (CA12 5TW) in the Lake District (ᗣ www.ospreywatch.co.uk ☎ 017687 78127), Rutland Water (LE15 8RN) in Rutland (ᗣ www.ospreys.org.uk ☎ 01572 737378) and Cors Dyfi (SY20 8SR), mid-Wales (ᗣ www.dyfiospreyproject.com ☎ 01654 781 414)

male do most of the fishing, so the crow posed little real danger – she was just letting it know who was boss.

Loch Garten is almost certainly the best place in Britain to see ospreys. The RSPB has a large, comfortable (if chilly at 6.30 or so on an April morning) hide that's roughly 250 metres from a nest site the same female has been using for the past 15 years. Ospreys return to the UK from West Africa or southern Europe in the spring, and once they've found a location they like for rearing chicks, they rarely go anywhere else. Home sweet home – though it's more like a second home.

When you see them with such ease, it's difficult to imagine that as recently as the 1980s, ospreys were rare in Britain, having been absent as breeding birds from 1916 until 1954. Today, some 250 pairs breed in Scotland every year, another 100 in England and Wales, and numbers are continuing to climb.

A few days after seeing the Loch Garten ospreys, I was cycling across the Dornoch Firth, having just gone through Tain and past the Glenmorangie Distillery (and somehow resisted the temptation to stop for a tour) when I spotted a massive bird hovering above the bridge on the far side of the firth. I say hovering, but it was right at the edge of what was possible for a bird of its size.

The osprey eventually dived down to the estuary, but pulled out at the last minute, and continued to scan from a height of some 20-30 metres. Eventually, it went again, and this time emerged with a fish for all its hard work. I can only assume it didn't have a mate waiting to be fed somewhere, because it took its prey to a boulder on the beach to feed in peace.

23 RUTTING RED DEER

BIG MOOR, CURBAR GAP, PEAK DISTRICT

Family friendly ★★★
The deer are easy to find, but don't get closer than 100 metres

Budget friendly ★★★★
Free if you go by yourself – the car park is pay and display, free to RSPB and National Trust members

Amateur friendly ★★★
Little expertise required, though red deer blend in surprisingly well with their environment

Best time of year
Mid-Sept-mid-Oct

From the Curbar Gap car park, it was a relatively easy 15-minute walk (a couple of small hills, nothing else) to the cairn marked on the Ordnance Survey map to the north and east. Once there, we got fabulous views over the expanse of Big Moor, now in late October the colour of a wheat field ready to be harvested.

It was 8am, and apart from a couple of hardy runners passed on the trail, we – myself and community ranger Bryony Thompson – were alone. But it was only when I heard a rumbling bellow, a stag announcing his claim to his harem, that I realised there were deer here, too. I scanned the depression of Big Moor with my binoculars, and suddenly I noticed groups everywhere – five here, ten there, feeding peacefully in the early morning light.

It was the end of the rutting season, so with most of the females already pregnant, the fight had gone out of the stags. I should have been here in late September or early October, when I might have seen so-called 'parallel walking', where the stags size each other up as they pass each other by, and possibly a proper clash of antlers if they decided to fight.

Big Moor is a natural amphitheatre, a huge shallow bowl where you can watch the deer from most sides. Bryony told me it's speculated they may come here because the setting amplifies the sound of the males' roaring, though there's good feeding here too.

DO IT YOURSELF

Curbar Gap car park is just outside the village of Curbar and marked on the Ordnance Survey map. From here, take the trail heading north-east for about 600-700 metres to the cairn overlooking Big Moor (also marked on the OS).

Alternatively, park on a layby on the B6054 (between Owler Bar and the junction with the A625) and head south towards the north side of Big Moor. After about 500 metres, you should find yourself overlooking the other side of Big Moor.

The Eastern Moors is an area of the Peak District managed in partnership by the National Trust and RSPB. The team runs guided walks, booking essential: ⌂ www.visit-eastern-moors.org.uk/plan-your-visit/whats-on.html ☎ 0114 2891543

There are many other places in Britain to see the red deer rut – try Richmond Park in London, Exmoor, Fountains Abbey in North Yorkshire, the Galloway Forest Park in south-west Scotland or the Isles of Arran, Jura and Rum in Scotland.

Later, from the north side of the moor, I walked along an easy track to the other side of the bowl – here two males were competing for a group of ten or so hinds. One was smaller and had lost one of his antlers, and it was the larger one who held sway, finally swaggering off with his harem, his head held high.

22 RETURNING MANX SHEARWATERS

SKOMER ISLAND, PEMBROKESHIRE

Family friendly ★★★

Potentially, but requires staying up until at least 11 or 11.30pm

Budget friendly ★★

It costs between £30-60 a night per person to stay on Skomer (half price for children) – it is cheaper in August and September, and all people staying on the island save on the usual landing fee (£10/£5)

Amateur friendly ★★★★

Easy to identify shearwaters from their calls

Best time of year

April-Sept

Toilets ✓

With some 316,000 breeding pairs on just 3km² of gently undulating, grassy terrain, Skomer Island is the world's Manx shearwater capital, but if you visit during the day, you won't see a single one – not alive, anyway. You'll find the wings and picked-clean carcasses of those that didn't

---

DO IT YOURSELF

Skomer is managed by the Wildlife Trust of South and West Wales. You don't have to be a member to spend the night there (or visit for the day), but it helps. They start taking bookings for night stays at the beginning of October, with members of the trust given first option. ☝ www.welshwildlife. org ☎ 01656 724100

Try to avoid the time around the full moon because Manx shearwater activity is greatly reduced due to increased risk of predation by gulls.

It's also possible to see Manx shearwaters on the island of Bardsey in North Wales. There is self-catering accommodation on the island or you can stay at the Bird Observatory. Bardsey Island Trust (☝ www. bardsey.org ☎ 08458 112233) or the observatory (☝ www.bbfo.org.uk ☎ 01626 773908)

make it home scattered across the island – an avian Whodunnit for any 'Inspector Oiseaus' out there.

Manx shearwaters are medium-sized seabirds, black on top and white underneath. They are excellent fliers, gliding on stiff wings low over the sea, and they spend long periods far away from land. They're a bit hopeless on terra firma, however. Their legs are set far back on their bodies, and the minute they hit dry land, they stagger about as if they've had a pint of scrumpy cider or three too many.

They must return to Skomer to take over egg or chick-tending duties from their partner, but if they come in daylight, great black-backed gulls pick them off, leaving just those carcasses. Instead, they return under darkness, and so – in order to see this – you have to spend the night on Skomer and only venture out once all daylight has gone.

You'll hear their harsh cry, which sounds like a cross between a raucous laugh and the anguished wail of a soul in purgatory, before you see them. It's said the Vikings thought the island of Rum, another breeding ground for them, must be inhabited by trolls such was the cacophonous noise they produced.

The birds call out to make contact with their mate, who is underground in one of the thousands of burrows that pock-mark the island. They land in a tangled heap, looking as dazed and confused as if they'd just been teleported off the *USS Enterprise*, then scramble towards their burrow. In truth, it's rather splendid in a slightly undignified way.

Come September, the pair and their chick (close to 1 million birds) fly this temporary home all the way across the Atlantic to the coasts of Argentina and Brazil, where they'll spend the winter.

© Dave Boyle

21 URBAN PEREGRINE FALCONS

NORWICH CATHEDRAL

Family friendly ★★★
Peregrine sightings almost guaranteed, but at quite a distance

Budget friendly ★★★★★
Nothing to pay

Amateur friendly ★★★★★
Experts on hand most of the time to help you spot the birds

Best time of year
March–July

Toilets ✓
Cafe ✓

© Hawk and Owl Trust

The day I pitched up to the Hawk and Owl Trust tent in the grounds of Norwich Cathedral in June 2017, the female peregrine was clinging to the spire, watching her only surviving chick flapping its wings in preparation for its first flight – it was expected to leave the nest and fledge within a week.

DO IT YOURSELF

The Hawk and Owl Trust has peregrine-watch projects at Norwich Cathedral and St John's Church (BA2 4AF) in Bath. Spotting scopes help you to see the peregrines close-up, and there's CCTV on the nests – in Norwich, you can even sit in the café and watch the antics of the chicks.

These projects run from mid-March towards the end of June or early July (whenever the chicks fledge). ⊕ hawkandowl.org ☎ 01328 850 590. Look out, too, for peregrines hunting – one sign is pigeons scattering or showing alarm.

The RSPB also runs a number of peregrine-watch initiatives – there's a good one at Symonds Yat in the Wye Valley in Gloucestershire, where you can watch rural peregrines hunting besides the spectacular limestone cliffs. ⊕ www.rspb.org.uk/groups/gloucestershire/places/316586

The female had laid four eggs, but only one chick made it to this stage – one didn't hatch, another chick died early of unknown natural causes and the third met a nasty end when the female got spooked while brooding her young – she accidentally flew off with the chick caught in her talons and dropped it. Who knew life for a city falcon could be so nasty, brutish and potentially short? In fact, the soap opera lives of the peregrines, which veer between cartoonish violence of *East Enders* and the tragedy of *Tess of the D'urbevilles*, are very well understood, thanks to the Hawk and Owl Trust.

The peregrines have nested on a specially installed platform, high up on the cathedral spire, since 2011, and are visible most days during the breeding season. Like soap opera fans, volunteers from the trust watch them on an almost daily basis and know their lives intimately.

The female, I was told, was a first-time mother, but hardly the Virgin Mary. Last year, she arrived in Norwich, having come all the way from Bath (the trust knows this because they ringed the female there when she was born), promptly ousting the tenant female who had four chicks at the time. The male, it seems, gets little say in who he mates with – his only job is to hunt and bring home food for the mother and the chicks.

He carried on feeding the old female's chicks, but normally this is a two-bird job, and he struggled. The new female killed one of them, and another died from some kind of parasitic infection – the theory is that he was taking straggler pigeons that may have borne a heavier parasite load than others, and this was then passed onto his offspring.

20 OTTER-SPOTTING

SHETLAND MAINLAND

Family friendly ★★
Not suitable for most children under 12 – it requires patience and doing what you're told

Budget friendly ★★
Costs £100 a day for an individual, £150 for a couple

Amateur friendly ★★★★★
The expert will find the otters for you

Best time of year
Otters are around all year, but much better weather in Shetland from May-Sept

Most encounters with otters in Britain are purely by chance. They can happen when and where you least expect it, but – conversely – you can spend a fortnight (as I did with my family) in a location such as Orkney, with all its perfect rocky shores, and not even catch a fleeting glimpse of an ottery tale.

Some years ago, my then six-year-old son saw one from our cottage while holidaying on Mull, and we were able to watch it for 15 minutes or so, and I once had a brief sighting while sea kayaking around Dinas Head in Pembrokeshire. I wouldn't recommend either method as giving you very good odds of success.

But there is a man who describes himself as 'Shetland's only dedicated full time otter watching guide' (he could probably substitute the UK for Shetland),

DO IT YOURSELF

John Campbell offers a range of otter-spotting packages. ✋ www.shetlandotters.com
☎ 01806 577 358

Scotland is the best place to see otters in Britain – Orkney is also good, as is much of the west coast.

In England, Shapwick Heath has a reputation of offering good otter sightings. ✋ avalonmarshes. org/explore/nature-reserves/shapwick-heath ☎ 01458 860120

and having enjoyed a morning with John Campbell, I would thoroughly recommend him as the best solution to the frustrated otter spotter.

What's more, for John, spotting the otter is just the start of it. Within 10 minutes of getting the scope out at a likely-looking voe (in Shetland, a term for a creek or inlet), John had already found one. It was on the far side of the voe, some 300-400 metres away, though it was easily visible in the scope. Job done, I thought, we can go and have some coffee and cake.

But John had other ideas. Circling round to the other side of the inlet where the otter was hunting, we moved from otter-spotting into all-out otter-stalking mode. John explained how, when the otter dived, we had roughly 30 seconds to cover as much ground as possible to get closer before it resurfaced and potentially noticed us.

We were running through fields, dodging gaudy orchids that grew like buttercups and diving for cover behind a dry stone wall as the half minute elapsed. Then, a quick look with the binoculars to see where the otter had got to, a short wait for it to dive, and we were off again.

After several such bursts, we were less than 50 metres from the unsuspecting animal, and we watched happily for some time as it came ashore and ate its catch. This may only be otter spotting, but it's the deluxe version.

© John Campbell

19 RETURNING STORM PETRELS

MOUSA, SHETLAND

Family friendly ★★

In mid-summer, trips don't start until 10.30pm and last until 12.30 or 1am

Budget friendly ★★

A 2½ hour trip would cost about £70 for a family of four

Amateur friendly ★★★★★

No specialist knowledge required

Best time of year

Late May-mid July

Standing by the huge stone broch, which was reminiscent in shape to the cooling tower of a power station, in Shetland's so-called 'simmer dim' – the late twilight experienced this far north – I could just about make out where Mousa's shoreline met the sea, but it was now nearing 11.30 at night, and, finally, it was starting to get dark. Mousa is roughly the same latitude north as Oslo, so

DO IT YOURSELF

Trips to Mousa are operated by the Mousa Boat and run from late May until mid-July. They leave at 10.30pm and last between 2 and 2.5 hours. You can also visit during the day – in the spring and summer, Arctic and great skuas and Arctic terns all breed here, and common (harbour) seals have their pups here in June. Trips leave from Sandsayre Pier, just outside of Sandwick, and must be booked in advance. ⌐ www.mousa.co.uk ☎ 07901 872339

Mousa is an RSPB Reserve ⌐ www.rspb.org/mousa ☎ 01950 460800

Storm petrels also nest on St Agnes and Gugh, in the Scilly Isles, on Lundy in the Bristol Channel, and Bardsey Island, off the Lleyn Peninsula in North Wales, but in much smaller numbers. They have only returned to Scilly and Lundy thanks to rat eradication programmes (rats ate their eggs).

in late June, just days after the summer solstice, it's light for about 20 hours a day.

As with the Manx shearwaters on Skomer (**Experience 22**), the wildlife we were waiting for would only appear under the cover of darkness. Now, finally, the birds began to return, announcing their presence with a series of churring, chattery calls and the fluttering of tiny wings – storm petrels, hardy, sparrow-sized seabirds coming back to their nests after days or weeks out at sea, locating their mates by calling out into the night and waiting for the other to respond.

I was standing by the broch, because this 2,300-year-old Iron Age roundhouse might not house people any more, but the crevices in its dry stone walls provide perfect nest sites for the storm petrels, making Mousa the most important location for the species in Britain today – nearly half of the breeding population, some 12,000 pairs, is found on this island. Elsewhere on Mousa (and other islands), they nest in boulder rubble, which the broch's stone construction mimics.

Like many of our seabirds, the breeding season is the almost the only time these birds are ever seen on dry land. For the rest of the year, and during the gale-lashed winter months, they live far out in the North Atlantic.

18 BOXING HARES

WALLASEA ISLAND

Family friendly ★★
Often hard to spot and can
spook easily

Budget friendly ★★★★★
Hare watching is generally free

Amateur friendly ★★
Knowing how to find them is
crucial

Best time of year
Almost any time of year –
March to May is good, though

There is something more than a little crazy about brown hares. Most wild animals don't scamper a quarter of a mile in one direction for no apparent good reason, make brief contact with a potential mate – or rival – then scamper back where it had come from. Only slightly dim springer spaniels and golden retrievers do that. But that's what I witnessed

DO IT YOURSELF

Wallasea Island (SS4 2HD) is in quite a remote location in south-east Essex, with the nearest big town being Southend-on-Sea. ☝ www.rspb.org/wallaseaisland ☎ 01268 498620

Buckenham Marshes (NR13 4HW) in Norfolk (☝ www.rspb.org/buckenhammarshes ☎ 01603 715191) and Thetford Forest (☝ www.forestryengland.uk/thetford-forest ☎ 0300 067 4500) in Suffolk also both recommended.

In my experience, the Forest of Bowland in Lancashire has some of the best populations in the country. Try Bleasdale Cottages (PR3 1UY), just outside the village of Bleasdale in the south-west of Bowland, where the farmland is also managed for breeding waders. ☎ 01995 61343

Havergate Island, in Suffolk, has a small population. ☝ www.rspb.org/havergateisland ☎ 01394 450732

on the windswept flats of Wallasea Island, a desolate amalgam of farmland, saltmarsh and mudflats in the River Crouch, the next major river up from the Thames.

It was late Marsh, and a cold biting wind blew over the low ground, while the hares were just beginning to get their blood lust up – they're not called 'Mad March Hares' for nothing. What I really wanted to witness was boxing hares, the behaviour in which females fight off potential suitors with their front paws because they're not ready to mate or he's not 'the one'. It's not, as is sometimes popularly supposed, two males fighting each other over a potential mate. But, I have to be honest – I didn't see it on this occasion, and nor have I ever witnessed it. I've watched hares all over the country, and somehow the boxing spectacle has always eluded me.

Like their close cousins, rabbits, brown hares are not properly native to Great Britain, having been brought here probably by the Romans some 2,000 years ago. They're Britain's fastest land mammal, with an estimated top speed of up to 70kph, and their fleetness of foot means they don't need to live in underground warrens (like rabbits do) to stay safe because their acceleration and speed can carry them away from danger. They graze in large arable fields, and consequently tend to be more common on the east side of Britain (where there's more arable farming) with East Anglia their particular stronghold.

Before you start looking for them, it's worth having an idea of how a hare differs from a rabbit – they're much larger, for a start, with a body length almost a third greater. They have longer hind legs (all the better to run away from you with) and longer, black-tipped ears (all the better to hear you with).

17 HUNTING GOLDEN EAGLES

HARRIS

Family friendly ★★★

Not a long walk, but sightings not guaranteed

Budget friendly ★★★★

Just the cost of getting to Harris

Amateur friendly ★★

Easy to mistake other birds for golden eagles

Best time of year

There are eagles here all year round, but Feb-April recommended

Golden eagles are sometimes described as Britain's last true symbol of wilderness. Here, they have been driven to our remotest mountain habitats, and they are very,

DO IT YOURSELF

The car park at Bowglass (Bhoga Glas) is easy to find. It's on the A859 some 10-12km north of Tarbert. The road descends down to Loch Seaforth and then passes the Scaladale outdoor centre. Bowglass is another 1-2km further on. The well-marked trail heads west from the car park. It's well-maintained, and though it's a continuous ascent, it's never steep.

There's also a golden eagle observatory in Glen Meavaig maintained by the North Harris Trust.
🖱 www.north-harris.org/north-harris/the-north-harris-eagle-observatory ☎ 01859 502222

The RSPB and others have created a self-guided Bird of Prey Trail for the Outer Hebrides.
🖱 www.hebridesbirdofpreytrail.co.uk

It's worth having some idea of how to identify golden eagles. Colour or markings are not reliable guides, but size and shape are – they are about the same size as white-tailed eagles (and therefore twice the size of buzzards or ravens), but their wings are slightly narrower than those of the white-tailed, their necks shorter and their tails longer.

very hard to see unless you're an expert birder, have an excellent guide or are extremely lucky. Even if you do see one (and can positively identify it), the chances are it's not much more than a speck in the lenses of your binoculars.

But there's one place in Britain where these odds are so spectacularly reversed it's been described as one of the best places to see golden eagles in the whole of Europe. The track that you walk up runs between four different eagle territories, and come here during the spring and early summer breeding season, according to Robin Reid of the RSPB, and there's a good chance even an average wildlife enthusiast will see between one and five eagles – both golden and white-tailed, which are also here in increasingly good numbers.

My experience of walking this trail in August confirmed the potential of the area. With my family, we saw two or three (we couldn't agree) golden eagles riding the air currents of the ridge of Mullach a' Ruisg, and this was with a grumpy three-year-old and even grumpier six-year-old, though they soon perked up when the eagles hoved into view.

Later, they returned to the car park with my partner while I carried on alone, and I saw a lone eagle plummet to the heather and boulder-strewn mountainside. I lost it for half a minute or so, and then it rose up with a body – a mountain hare, I guessed, their main prey items on Harris – suspended from its talons. It climbed slowly with the hare, which must have been half its weight, then took it down to the other side of the ridge and out of sight.

16 FEEDING RED KITES

BWLCH NANT YR ARIAN

Family friendly ★★★★★
Easy viewing of beautiful birds of prey

Budget friendly ★★★★★
You have to pay for the car parking, but nothing else

Amateur friendly ★★★★★
Absolutely – look out for the classic forked tail of the red kites

Best time of year
All year round, but greater numbers in the winter

Toilets ✓
Cafe ✓

They might not be everybody's cup of tea, but personally I'm a big fan of vultures – squabbling over kills like siblings from East Enders and then feasting as if they were at the court of King Henry VIII. There's not

DO IT YOURSELF

Bwlch Nant yr Arian (SY23 3AB) is easy to find as it's on the A44 between Aberystwyth and Llangurig. ⌐ www.naturalresources.wales/bwlchnantyrarian?lang=en ☎ 01970 890453

There are a number of other red kite feeding stations in Britain – also in Wales is Gigrin Farm (LD6 5BL), near Rhayader. ⌐ www.gigrin.co.uk; 01597 810 243. In south-west Scotland, there's Bellymack Hill Farm (DG7 2PJ), on the Galloway Red Kite Trail in Dumfries & Galloway (⌐ www.bellymackhillfarm.co.uk); and in Central Scotland there's Argaty Red Kites (FK16 6EJ), in Perthshire. ⌐ www.argatyredkites.co.uk ☎ 01786 841373

Other locations where red kites are likely to be sighted include: Derwent Valley, Gateshead; Harewood House, Yorkshire; Top Lodge, Northamptonshire and the Chilterns Area of Outstanding Natural Beauty.

much room for niceties when you live off scavenged carcasses. We don't have vultures in the Britain, but we do have the next best thing: red kites.

With a wing span of up to 2.2 metres – that's more than the height of any normal human – the red kite is a big and impressive bird, with a rich, russet plumage and a distinctive forked tail. Many people will have seen them circling over motorways such as the M4 or M42, looking for roadkill; they're even common visitors to towns such as Reading these days, and in the Chilterns, some people feed them the remains of their Sunday roast.

But come tea time – 3pm in the summer, 2pm in the winter – visitors to the Natural Resources Wales centre of Bwlch Nant yr Arian near Machynlleth get a real treat, as tens, and at times hundreds, of these birds turn up to pick over butchers' offcuts and bones.

The kites know exactly what's coming, so they start circling over the lake near the visitor centre half an hour or more before the food is put out. By the time it's nearly tea time, the sky is awash with birds, prowling the air space like modern-day pterosaurs. There's plenty of food to go round, but that doesn't stop the occasional aerial scrap between rivals.

The red kite has experienced extraordinary highs and lows over the past few centuries. Once common scavengers in towns and cities where they acted like street cleaners, they then almost disappeared from Britain entirely because of persecution by gamekeepers who hated them for taking pheasants and other gamebirds. They hung on in Wales, but only just; reintroduction programmes all over the country then brought them back from the brink.

15 HUNTING ORCAS

Family friendly ★

You'll need patience – expect to be disappointed

Budget friendly ★★★

If you want the best chance of seeing one, use local guides

Amateur friendly ★★★

They are very distinctive animals, but knowing where to look is crucial

Best time of year

April-Sept

I s there such a thing as the world's ultimate predator? The top dog of all top dogs? Well, not really, but – if pushed (it's a bit like asking who's the greatest-ever athlete), I'd have to say the killer whale or orca. Put it like this, it's the only species on the planet known to hunt great white sharks and eat their livers (probably without fava beans and a nice Chianti).

They are large, ranging in size from 5-8 metres (and the largest male on record was hand's length short of being 10 metres), highly intelligent members of the dolphin family, and they eat everything from herring and salmon to the calves of grey and humpback whales. Everything, that is, apart from us.

Shetland is without doubt the best place to see killer whales in Britain – there are prodigious quantities of herring here at certain times of year, and abundant grey and harbour seals (another favourite prey item) all year round.

My own experience of visiting the islands resulted in a fantastic but slightly frustrating week chasing after them. 'You should have been here yesterday,'

DO IT YOURSELF

Shetland Wildlife has the best local knowledge on where the orcas are, including a Facebook page where people can record the latest sightings. ✆ www.shetlandwildlife.co.uk ☎ 01950 460939 ✆ www.facebook.com/groups/shetlandorcasightings

There are numerous flights to Shetland these days, mainly originating from Aberdeen, Edinburgh or Inverness. ✆ www.shetland.org

I was told, not quite at every turn; or in one case, 'You should have been here this morning.' I visited Fair Isle (an island south of Shetland) one day, and on my return, picked up a message, from local wildlife guide Hugh Harrop, that had been left on my voicemail about 15 minutes earlier. 'There are killer whales off Sumburgh Head,' he said. 'Get down here if you can.' I'd been flying over Sumburgh Head at almost the exact moment he'd left the message – if I'd looked down, I might have seen them.

But I have seen killer whales in the wild, off Vancouver, and there is something about their piebald beauty, those huge blunt heads and the males' enormous dorsal fins that sets them apart from every living thing on the planet. They're not subtle.

Seeing killer whales in Shetland is a matter of luck however – if sightings were in any way reliable, then it would be in my top 10 for certain. Around Shetland, I've heard stories of them hunting seals by attempting to beach themselves on rocks (akin to the famous footage of orcas going after sealions off Península Valdés in Argentina in David Attenborough's 1990 series, *The Trials of Life*) and of one occasion when a group was seen hoovering up eider ducks in Lerwick Harbour.

14 EMERGING PIPISTRELLE BATS

LACOCK ABBEY, NEAR CHIPPENHAM

Family friendly ★★★★
Hundreds of bats emerging from gargoyles

Budget friendly ★★★★
Walks run by the National Trust charge a small fee

Amateur friendly ★★★★★
Walks are led by an expert who's been monitoring the bats for many years

Best time of year
July & August

A crepuscular gloom had descended on the grounds of Lacock Abbey while I stood waiting with Tony Brazier and his observer team from Wiltshire Bat Group. As the clock crept closer to 9pm, we kept our eyes firmly fixed on the old stone gargoyles that studded the outside of the octagonal building on the east wing of the abbey. 'Any minute now,' Tony murmured.

It was just before the hour mark when the first bat appeared, sprouting out of the gargoyle like a plant bursting into flower and then quickly disappearing up and away for a night-time's feeding. A minute or two passed, and another one had clearly decided it was dark enough to make a move; if they leave

DO IT YOURSELF

Lacock Abbey (SN15 2LG) is owned and run by the National Trust and is not usually open to the public in the evenings. But the trust organises at least two bat walks, guided by Tony Brazier, every year, usually in July and August. Lacock Abbey 🖰 www.nationaltrust.org.uk/lacock-abbey-fox-talbot-museum-and-village ☎ 01249 730459

For other bat-related activities, see Bat detecting (Experience 63) and Greater horseshoe bats (Experience 66).

too early, they are potentially vulnerable to predation by sparrowhawks. It took a while, but soon they were streaming out, one after the other in rapid succession as if a small child were blowing black bubbles into the summer air.

There is something deliciously appropriate about bats leaving their sleeping quarters (which is actually the space between the ceiling and the roof) via a gothic contrivance such as a gargoyle, but that's not the only reason why this is such a life-affirming experience. Huge numbers of females spend the spring and summer here raising their pups, with 1,037 being the most that Tony has ever counted in a single night.

Lacock's grounds themselves are a bat idyll. The parkland habitat provides partially wooded areas for the pipistrelles, while open grassland areas are good for other species. Down by the River Avon, insects milled like taxis round Piccadilly Circus, providing a bonanza for Daubenton's bats, which feed (like no other British bat) by skimming low over the surface of the water in lazy arcs.

After Tony had counted all the pips – they'd all emerged by about 9.30 on the night for a count of just over 900 – he took me on a bat walk around the abbey. Listening to their calls on the bat detector, he explained how their increasing rapidity indicated that a bat was getting closer to its prey, ending with a noise that sounded like someone blowing a raspberry – the end of another insect, a meal for the bat.

13 PUFFINS ON PARADE

HERMANESS NNR

Family friendly ★★★
It's a bit of a hike from the carpark to the cliffs, and – parents with young children, beware – they are very high cliffs

Budget friendly ★★★★
Apart from the cost of getting to Shetland

Amateur friendly ★★★★★
You'll know a puffin when you see one

Best time of year
April-July

Toilets ✓

© James Fair

There are countless places in Britain to see puffins (many people's favourite seabird, surely) but there are perhaps four stand-out locations – Skomer Island, off the coast of West Wales, the Treshnish Isles, off the island of Mull in the Inner Hebrides, the Isle of May in the Outer Firth of Forth and Hermaness on Shetland, which is almost but not quite the northernmost point of the whole of the British Isles (that title goes to the appropriately-named rock, Out Stack).

The reason I pick these three locations is because you can get so close to puffins that are completely unfazed by humans. Unlike most other seabirds, which nest on cliff faces, puffins prefer a nice underground burrow in which to lay their eggs and raise chicks, and they usually access their home from ground level, which they must therefore share with whatever else is using it – us, for example. On Skomer, I've seen them practically run between someone's legs as they scurry back to their burrow with a beakful of sandeels.

But Hermaness is my puffin top spot because of the drama of the scenery. From the carpark and visitor centre, you walk up gently sloping rough moorland (look out for great skuas, or 'bonxies' – **Experience 71**) until you reach cliffs that are, at their highest point, 180m above the sea. The puffins have their burrows at the top of this cliff, and gather right at the edge in small, sociable groups as if gossiping about the indiscretions of Mavis at number 15.

DO IT YOURSELF

Hermaness NNR (ZE2 9EQ) is managed by Scottish Natural Heritage. Find a spot on the cliff-edge, but don't directly approach the puffins – let them come to you. If a puffin is hesitating about going into its burrow (because you're in the way), it could be mugged by a great skua. ⌂ www.nature.scot

Skomer is managed by the Wildlife Trust of South and West Wales. ⌂ www.welshwildlife. org ☎ 01656 724100

The Treshnish Isles are off the west coast of Mull in the Inner Hebrides. Southern Hebrides Scotland website has details of all the operators that run trips there (from Oban, Fionnport on Mull, Ulva Ferry and Iona). ⌂ www.southernhebrides.com

Other good places to see puffins include the Farne Islands (see experience 41), the Isle of May and Bempton Cliffs.

Some fly in, others fly out, and it's a constant whirr of activity as they go about their business. On my only visit to Hermaness, the sun was out and it was a beautiful and improbably warm day, and I lay on the grass just metres from a group of puffins who seemed to care not a jot that I was watching them. I really cannot imagine a more relaxing way to spend an hour or two.

12 COMMON DOLPHINS

IRISH SEA (OFF PEMBROKESHIRE)

Family friendly ★★★
Children usually love boat trips, but these are often long and some go far offshore

Budget friendly ★
Costs can be £60 for adults, £30 for children, for 2-3 hour boat trips

Amateur friendly ★★★★
Sharp eyesight helpful, but no specialist knowledge required

Best time of year
Trips only run April-Sept

Common dolphins, as their name implies, are indeed common around much of Britain's Atlantic coastline – indeed, they range widely throughout the world. They are smaller creatures than the dolphins everyone thinks of as Flipper – bottlenose dolphins, the ones with uniform grey bodies and large, hooked dorsal fins. Common dolphins, in

---

DO IT YOURSELF

Falcon Boats run common dolphin and other wildlife trips out of St Davids (🖰 www.falconboats.co.uk; 07494 141764), as do Thousand Islands Expeditions (🖰 thousandislands.co.uk ☎ 01437 721721) and Dale Sailing out of Martin's Haven, near Marloes (🖰 www.pembrokeshire-islands.co.uk ☎ 01646 603123).

Arisaig Marine runs trips from Arisaig out to the Small Isles of Eigg, Muck and Rum, and (according to the Sea Watch Foundation) is especially good at finding dolphins and whales. 🖰 www.arisaig.co.uk ☎ 01687 450224

Find out more about all dolphins from, and report any sightings, to the Sea Watch Foundation. 🖰 www.seawatchfoundation.org.uk ☎ 01407 832892

contrast, have an hourglass marking, which may be cream, grey or yellow, on their flank that begins just behind their eyes and goes as far back as their dorsal fin.

But while they may live up to their name in terms of numbers and geographic spread, that doesn't make them easy to find. There are four coastal groups of bottlenose dolphins in Britain that live in fairly defined locations (East Scotland, Cardigan Bay, off the coast of Cornwall and the Hebrides), and there are boat trips that go out most days of the summer with a good chance of seeing them. Common dolphins, however, are more nomadic and live further out to sea, and in general, you stumble across a group of these animals by chance.

But some of my most memorable encounters with wildlife of any kind have been with common dolphins. Once, on a trip out of St David's, in Pembrokeshire, we were returning from a visit to the gannet colony on Grassholm when a group of 10 or 15 dolphins appeared out of nowhere. They surrounded the boat, bobbing and weaving in the bow wave and to the side like the horses on a merry-go-round, all effortless grace and joyful energy. They stayed less than 10 minutes, vanishing in a trice as if they'd just been called home for their tea.

On another occasion, somewhere off the Small Isles in the Inner Hebrides, we found a smaller group of five of six individuals. They took to bow-riding at the front of the boat, and I remember staring down at the blow-hole of a dolphin that appeared to keep pace with us without making any effort at all.

These types of encounters are as predictable as a chance meeting with a friend in a strange city. But it's that very improbability that makes them even more rewarding.

11 STARLING MURMURATION

HAM WALL RSPB RESERVE, ASHCOTT

Family friendly ★★★★
Yes – but the best murmurations occur in sub-zero (or nearly sub-zero) temperatures

Budget friendly ★★★★★
There's a small car park charge for non-members of the RSPB

Amateur friendly ★★★★★
Just look to the skies – you can't mistake a murmuration for anything else

Best time of year
Jan-Feb

Toilets ✓

I f you've never seen a starling murmuration yourself, you only have to watch a clip on YouTube to realise that this is something completely different to any other wildlife encounter you can have in Britain. I'd say it's more like viewing a modern art installation –

DO IT YOURSELF

Starlings only gather in large numbers to roost during the winter, and the best months are January and February. You want to be in position by about 3 or 3.15 in January, 4pm in February – the later in the year you go, the later that dusk will be. Ham Wall RSPB Reserve (BA6 9SX) ⌖ www.rspb.org/hamwall ☎ 01458 860494 or try the 'Starling Hotline' (☎ 07866 554142) which tells you where the starlings are roosting at that time.

Other well-known locations for starling murmurations include Aberystwyth and Brighton piers (in the latter case, the derelict west one), Leighton Moss RSPB Reserve (LA5 0SW) in Lancashire, Fen Drayton Lakes (CB24 4SR) in Cambridgeshire and Gretna Green – this last one is said to move around, and is currently best viewed from the B721 to the west of Rigg.

A starling murmuration website maps all recorded sightings, so you can find the one closest to you – it is hard to say how current all the information is, however. ⌖ www.starlingsintheuk.co.uk

in the sky.

But what is a murmuration? During the winter months, and especially in very cold weather, starlings – small, glossy-coated songbirds about the size of a blackbird – gather in flocks comprising hundreds of thousands of individuals as dusk falls, and these flocks create optical illusions of fluid shapes that change and transform in front of you. In a sense, the fact they are starlings becomes irrelevant.

A cold and bright winter's day produces the best murmurations, a lovely time to go for a walk in itself. At Ham Wall, people gather there in their hundreds, and the sense of shared anticipation between people of all ages always reminds me of the atmosphere before a big sporting event. Just without any aggro or meat pies.

Having said that, one of the best murmurations I've ever seen was at Gloucester railway station – a small flock of probably only a few thousand starlings shape-shifted just a few hundred metres away for five or ten minutes as if dancing to some kind of inaudible music. It came from nowhere and was completely unexpected. No one else appeared to see it.

Why starlings behave in this way is fascinating, too. They will have been feeding in smaller groups during the day, and as they fly to their shared roost site for the night, they are vulnerable to predators such as peregrine falcons. By bunching together, scientists believe they make it harder to be picked off.

A sunny day is better because the better visibility increases the risks of predation, so you get bigger flocks, while very cold weather (especially if there's been a prolonged spell of it) means there will be more birds around, because many hundreds of thousands may come here to escape the even colder climes of continental Europe.

10 PINE MARTEN HIDE

ROTHIEMURCHUS ESTATE, CAIRNGORMS NP

Family friendly ★★★★★
A chance to watch one of Britain's shyest carnivores from a comfortable hide

Budget friendly ★★★
An evening in a pine marten hide can cost as little as £20

Amateur friendly ★★★★★
No chance of mistaking a pine marten for anything else

Best time of year
Spring, summer and autumn

Toilets ✓

It was almost too easy, too comfortable. We were happily standing around in a heated shed with large, full-height windows on either side that looked out onto brightly illuminated grassy banks. On one side, a tree and what looked like a large bird table rustically but solidly constructed from offcuts and branches, and on the other, some rocks with crevices and a narrow walkway between them and the glass.

DO IT YOURSELF

Speyside Wildlife organises trips to Rothiemurchus Estate hide. ⌨ www.speysidewildlife. co.uk ☎ 01479 812498

Aigas Field Centre (IV4 7AD), near Inverness, also has a pine marten hide. ⌨ www.aigas. co.uk ☎ 01463 782443

Glenloy Lodge (PH33 7PD), near Fort William, offers pine marten-watching evenings. ⌨ glenloywildlife.co.uk ☎ 01397 712700

You can expect to see pine martens and other wildlife at Dunchraigaig House B&B (PA31 8RG), near Kilmartin in Argyll. ⌨ dunchraigaig.co.uk ☎ 01546 605300

Many exhilarating wildlife encounters either necessitate life being difficult or uncomfortable – getting up far too early while it's dark and the rest of the family is asleep, for example, or being cold or wet. How, I wondered, could this evening (it wasn't even especially late – around 8.30pm in early May) ever provide an immersive and memorable experience?

We'd entered the hide just as it was getting dark, and John – our guide for the evening – explained that this was to make sure we were inside before any of the animals we hoped to see that night roused themselves for supper, and so we didn't scare them away. We could carry on talking, he said, but we should keep our voices low, and with luck we'd see plenty of badgers and – everybody's real target – a pine marten.

Pine martens are members of the mustelid family, and so related to both badgers and otters, neither of which they resemble a great deal – they are more similar to their smaller relatives, the stoats and the weasels though larger than both of them. They have the same sinuous long bodies, bushier tales – more like a fox's – and elfin-like, butter-wouldn't-melt faces, that some would argue belie their real nature. Including the tail, they can be up to 0.8m long – not much smaller than a fox, but with a low-slung carriage. One of

their most distinguishing features is the pale custard-yellow bib on their chest, which contrasts with the dark chestnut-brown colour of the rest of their fur. They're excellent climbers, and sleep, nest and even hunt in trees.

They are both incredibly rare in Britain and naturally elusive. While there is a small population in Wales (the subject of a programme to boost numbers by moving animals from Scotland) and occasional sightings in Northumberland, Shropshire and North Yorkshire, your only real chance of seeing one is north of the border. They're not common here, either; a survey from 2012 suggested a maximum of 3,500 across Scotland, though numbers are increasing.

But despite their natural shyness (in previous centuries, they were subjected to extensive persecution by gamekeepers because they were blamed for taking pheasants and other gamebirds), they can be tempted out into the open. Some operators in Scotland swear by peanut butter and even jam sandwiches – they have a sweet tooth, though there's a view that such highly refined carbs aren't great for a wild animal – but Rothiemurchus says the one thing pine martens can't resist is a nice raw egg.

So along with some peanuts, there was an egg on the bird table, and now we just had to wait. It didn't take long for the first badgers to arrive, shuffling cautiously into view with their snouts low to the ground, hoovering up the peanuts and sniffing out spoonfuls of peanut butter that had also been liberally placed in cracks and elsewhere. A wood mouse provided additional

entertainment, scampering among the rocks in a constant state of nervous tension.

Then came the pine marten, first to take some peanuts from the ground, casually chomping its way through this part of the smorgarsbord, but it was no more than a starter. It disappeared for five minutes or so, and then came a call from the other side of the hide. 'It's back,' someone whispered. We moved round, and there it was, effortlessly bounding through the short grass and up onto the bird table. One quick look around and it delicately picked it up in its teeth, leapt down onto the grass and waltzed off into the night.

There are no other truly predatory land carnivores you can have such a close and sustained sighting of in Britain – encounters with foxes, stoats and weasels are mainly random affairs, and while I would love to see a wildcat (**Experience 95**) in the wild, they are extremely rare and even more elusive than pine martens.

There's something else – recent studies from Ireland have shown how, where grey and red squirrels co-exist, pine martens prey disproportionately on the non-native greys, aiding conservation efforts to help native reds. It's a great example of how predators are key components of ecosystems – we may be fascinated by their hunting abilities, but we should also value them for maintaining the natural order.

PINE MARTEN HIDE

9 MARSH HARRIER FOOD PASS

LEIGHTON MOSS RSPB RESERVE

Family friendly ★★★
Observing marsh harriers from a distance not easy for younger children

Budget friendly ★★★
Entrance to Leighton Moss isn't free, unless you're a member of the RSPB or travel there by bike or public transport!

Amateur friendly ★★
Being able to identify a marsh harrier is a fairly critical skill

Best time of year
April-July

Toilets ✓
Cafe ✓

I was overlooking the vast wetland expanse of Ham Wall RSPB Reserve in the Somerset Levels, an area of Britain that has earned a reputation as the Camargue of the UK. It was April, and I was with my friend, Pete and the warden Steve Hughes, and we were ostensibly there to listen to one of the country's most secretive birds, the bittern, which makes a strange booming noise during the breeding season (**Experience 57**).

Suddenly, Steve spotted a male marsh harrier, a bird of prey about the size of a buzzard, but less chunky, with a longer tail and narrower, black-tipped wings. 'I think he's caught something,' Steve said. 'Wonder where the female is.'

Marsh harriers, as their name suggests, are birds of wetland habitats, and because there aren't many trees in this type of environment, they nest on the ground. When the male catches something – and they take a wide range of prey, including frogs, small mammals and birds such as moorhens – he's generally either looking to impress a female with whom he can mate or provision her with food while she's incubating eggs or to feed to the chicks.

But he can't carry the meal back to a safely located nest high up in a tree, because there isn't one, and if he carries it back to where the female is sitting

DO IT YOURSELF

Leighton Moss is an excellent place to see marsh harriers – it has 5 or 6 pairs breeding here in a relatively small area, and if you're not guaranteed to see a food pass, then sightings of the birds themselves are pretty reliable during the breeding season from April to July. I even saw one (from no more than 50 yards or so away) as I was cycling away from the reserve, which was pretty spectacular in itself.

Leighton Moss (LA5 0SW) 🖱 www.rspb.org/leightonmoss ☎ 01524 701601. A family of four can expect to get into the reserve for less than £20 (it will vary depending on the age of the kids).

Ham Wall (BA6 9SX) in the Somerset Levels also offers virtually guaranteed sightings of marsh harriers. 🖱 www.rspb.org/hamwall ☎ 01458 860494

Another classic location is Minsmere (IP17 3BY) in Suffolk. 🖱 www.rspb.org/minsmere ☎ 01728 648281

All three reserves have visitor centres that are open during the spring at normal hours – the ones at Leighton Moss and Minsmere are quite substantial, including cafes serving hot meals, while Ham Wall's is much smaller, but during the spring there will always be people on hand to tell you where to go and how to give yourself the best chance of see marsh harriers. Some of these reserves will also do guided walks (or 'Dates with nature' as the RSPB calls them), so it's worth ringing up and finding out if they have got anything coming up.

on the ground, he risks giving away the location of vulnerable eggs or chicks to a potential predator.

Instead, she joins him in the air, and this is where it gets interesting. Even though our pair were some 300-400 metres away, through our binoculars we could clearly see them approach each other. At the last minute, the female turned upside down in mid-air and extended her talons to seize the prize that he was just about to drop into her grasp. He let go, but something went wrong and the animal – Steve told me later he thought it was a frog – plummeted to the ground. 'Oops,' I remarked. 'Is that meant to happen?'

About a week later, I was at Leighton Moss, a similar wetland habitat just north of Morecambe in Lancashire, and this time the marsh harriers I was watching were successful in completing the fabled food pass. They circled each other for a short time, then the female flew up to the male from below and – at the last minute – you could clearly see her twisting in the air so that their talons were almost meeting. It was a bit like watching a pair of trapeze artists performing a stunt where one flings themselves from the trapeze in mid-air and is caught by the other in their hands.

Roy Dennis, one of Britain's top experts on birds of prey, believes there may be another reason why marsh harriers go to all the trouble of performing

a circus act for the relatively simple process of passing food from one to the other, besides not revealing the location of the nest. As with most raptors, the female marsh harrier is quite a bit larger than the male. Apart from the sterling work he does providing her (and possibly another mate) with food, he plays no part in bringing up the chicks, and she doesn't really want him around – so, he's quite happy not having too much contact with her because it reduces the possibility she might attack him.

8 RED SQUIRRELS

HAWESWATER HOTEL

Family friendly ★★★★★
Enjoy a drink or a meal in the hotel grounds and watch squirrels at the same time

Budget friendly ★★★★
The only thing you'll have to buy is a drink

Amateur friendly ★★★★★
Hard to misidentify a red squirrel

Best time of year
Spring, summer or a warm autumn day – you'll want to sit outside

Toilets ✓
Restaurant/bar ✓

The day I visited the Haweswater Hotel, I'd been working with a local photographer who'd been taking shots and videoing interviews for a magazine piece I was putting together on the wildlife of the Lake District. We'd just been down the road at the RSPB's Haweswater Reserve, at the time the location for England's solitary golden eagle, which subsequently disappeared and is now presumed to have died.

It was mid-afternoon, we were pretty much done for the day but a sign outside the hotel suggesting we might see some red squirrels there was tempting. The afternoon sunlight was soft and pretty, and we wondered whether this might be a good place to get some squirrel shots for the feature. And perhaps have a well-earned drink.

We didn't have to wait long. There were plenty of feeders crammed full of hazelnuts, and to reach them, the squirrels either had to run across the neatly trimmed lawn in that skippy-bouncy gait that few other mammals can imitate or negotiate the perfectly trimmed hedge. Showing absolutely no fear of the photographer, Ashley, they were perfect subjects for surely some of the easiest wildlife images ever taken. One squirrel emerged from raiding a feeder looking as if he'd just pilfered the lunch-club fund.

Two men, drinking pints after hiking over from Ullswater via High

DO IT YOURSELF

The Haweswater Hotel (CA10 2RP) is on the east side of Haweswater, on the eastern fringes of the Lake District itself. ⌁ www.haweswaterhotel.com ☎ 01931 713235

Also in the Lake District, try the narrow strip of woodland just outside Keswick that follows the course of the River Greta – start at Threlkeld Bridge (marked on the OS map). There are bird and squirrel feeders on your left after you've been walking for about five minutes. Whinlatter Forest Park (CA12 5TW) is another good bet. ⌁ www.forestryengland.uk/whinlatter ☎ 01768 778469

In the south of England, Brownsea is one of the best places to go to see red squirrels – it's a small island, and sightings of red squirrels are virtually guaranteed. Ferries leave from The Quay, on Poole Harbour. ⌁ www.brownseaislandferries.com ☎ 01929 462383

On Anglesey, Newborough Forest is also a great place to see red squirrels with encounters easy to come by. ⌁ www.redsquirrels.info/about/view-squirrels ☎ 07966 150847

There's a good population of red squirrels on the Sefton coast north of Liverpool. Try National Trust Formby (L37 1LJ) ⌁ www.nationaltrust.org.uk/formby ☎ 01704 878591

In Scotland, almost anywhere in lower elevations of the Cairngorms is good. Boat of Garten is recommended. ⌁ www.boatofgarten.com/community/local-wildlife

In the Scottish lowlands, the Scottish Wildlife Trust's Stenhouse Wood is recommended. ⌁ scottishwildlifetrust.org.uk/reserve/stenhouse-wood ☎ 0131 312 7765

Street, looked on with amusement. 'The squirrels are so close they'll be able to put them on the cover of a magazine,' one remarked to his friend. 'Funny you should say that,' I thought.

I'm not sure whether it's their lovely russet coats and tufted ears or because we know them to be Britain's native (as opposed to foreign) squirrel, but there's no disputing the charm of the red. Perhaps it's that bushy tail, so much bushier than its grey cousin's. In any case, it's true, they do look remarkably good on the cover of a magazine.

In fact, we had already seen red squirrels that day. I'd met Simon O'Hare, from Red Squirrels Northern England, in a small woodland on the old Threlkeld railway line just to the east of Keswick. He said they were easy to spot there, but there was a catch – we should be there by 6.30. 'We're less likely to be disturbed by walkers then,' he explained in an email.

After a short walk, we stopped and waited by a feeder in verdant woodland. The place was a hive of bird activity, but for 20 minutes or so it was definitely

lacking any squirrel activity. Then they appeared, two of them, one chasing the other over the mossy ground and up a tree. There they continued their spat for five minutes or so, until they tired of the unnecessary histrionics and disappeared. Though they were only 20 metres away, Ashley said they were too far away to get any decent photos. Hence why that sign outside the hotel advertising red squirrels tempted us.

Of course, the Lake District isn't the only place to see red squirrels in Britain. There are many excellent sites in Scotland where greys have never reached, so the reds are unaffected – where the two species do mix, reds frequently die out, because greys are carriers of a disease which is fatal for them, but which leaves the non-native, American squirrels unharmed. Some of the best strongholds in England are islands – Anglesey, Brownsea (in Poole Harbour) and the Isle of Wight, for example – which greys have never reached.

In the north of England – Cumbria, Northumberland and a few parts of Durham and Lancashire – they largely hang on by their tiny front paws thanks to the work of a small army of voluntary trappers and shooters who keep the greys at bay. But for the most part in these counties, you have to work hard for your squirrel fix, and even then, it's not guaranteed – except at the Haweswater Hotel.

7 PLUNGE-DIVING GANNETS

NOSS NNR

Family friendly ★★★★★
Comfortable boat with on-board facilities

Idiot friendly ★★★★★
Hard to miss plunge-diving gannets

Budget friendly ★
A family of four could expect to pay about £140 for a 2½ hour trip

Best time of year
April-Sept

Toilet ✓

Whoosh! Whoosh! Whoosh! There were seabirds all around me, diving like feathered spears and hitting the water at speeds of up to 100kph. Though capable of submerging down to 10 metres, these were resurfacing quickly, bobbing back up like corks, so whatever they were fishing for must have been close to the surface. Then they were off, having already swallowed their catch, back into the air to search for more prey.

With a wingspan of up to two metres, the northern gannet is Britain's largest seabird, but that doesn't begin to do justice to what a spectacular creature it is. During the breeding season, gannets live in large colonies around our coast, with most concentrated in Scotland, though there are also large 'gannetries' off the coast of Pembrokeshire in Wales and on Yorkshire's Bempton Cliffs.

The largest colony in the UK – Bass Rock, in the mouth of the Firth of Forth – is home to an incredible 75,000 pairs of gannets, though the rock itself covers only three hectares, about the size of three large international rugby fields. Or put it another way, that's two and a half nests for every square metre on the island. Because of the amazing concentration of gannets on this tiny volcanic plug of rock, it's where the species gets its scientific name, *Morus bassanus*.

I was watching my gannets in a boat just off Noss National Nature Reserve, an island off another island (Bressay) directly opposite Shetland's main town

DO IT YOURSELF

Shetland Seabird Tours offers daily boat trips to Noss between May and October, though the best gannet action is probably only up until the end of August. ✐ www.shetlandseabirdtours. com ☎ 07767 872260

You can also visit Noss itself on foot. First, you must take a ferry from Lerwick to Bressay (www. shetland.gov.uk/ferries/timetable.asp), then drive across the island. From here, a small inflatable boat, operated by Scottish Natural Heritage, takes you the short hop across the water to Noss; the Noss ferry runs from May to the end of August (not Mondays or Thursdays or in bad weather), and it's recommended you phone the ferry number before setting out. ☎ 0800 107 7818. ✐ www.visitscotland.com/info/see-do/noss-national-nature-reserve-p246931

Britain's (and indeed the world's) largest colony of northern gannets is Bass Rock, in the outer reaches of the Firth of Forth. The Scottish Seabird Centre (EH39 4SS), based in North Berwick, runs various trips out to both Bass Rock and the Isle of May (which is home to breeding puffins). ✐ seabird.org/visit/boats/10/22 ☎ 01620 890 202

Bempton Cliffs (YO15 1JF) is an RSPB reserve. ✐ www.rspb.org/bemptoncliffs ☎ 01262 422212. Yorkshire Coast Nature runs workshops at Bempton teaching the basics of how to capture dramatic images of gannets in flight. ✐ www.yorkshirecoastnature.co.uk ☎ 01723 865498

Grassholm is an island about 15km off the coast of South Pembrokeshire. You can't land on it, but Dale Sailing operate trips out of Marten's Haven, just outside the village of Marloes. ✐ www. pembrokeshire-islands.co.uk ☎ 01646 603123

Voyage of Discovery also run whale and dolphin-spotting expeditions which stop by Grassholm. ✐ www.ramseyisland.co.uk/the-islands/grassholm ☎ 01437 721 911

and port, Lerwick. With 12,000 pairs of gannets here in the breeding season (roughly March to October), this is a relatively small colony, but with its brooding sandstone cliffs, stained white by seabird excrement and rising to 181 metres, it's a dramatic place to watch them. The boat takes you right into the action, so there can be gannets 20 or 30 metres above your head while dozens of others plunge all around you.

I picked out one gannet and watched it carefully for a minute or two. It circled round in a wide arc and then headed into the wind so that it was almost hovering, kestrel-like, before it fell. It quickly accelerated as it dived, its wings outstretched to provide control and stability. At the last minute – just a few metres above the water – it sheathed them in one beautiful, fluid movement so that the bird hit the water with as streamlined a profile as

possible. I could watch that moment again and again and again. I frequently have.

The beauty of gannets is that you can be walking along a coastal path or even at a beach and you see them. I've watched plunge-diving gannets while building sandcastles with my children at Whitesands, just outside St David's in Pembrokeshire. Theoretically, you could be very far out at sea, as well – a small percentage of the gannets nesting at Bass Rock regularly visit Dogger Bank, some 300km to the east, in order to forage.

What's more, gannets are closely related to birds such as the blue-footed and masked boobies found halfway across the world in the Pacific Ocean, and these birds dive in exactly the same way. The spectacle in the northernmost reaches of the British Isles is almost exactly the same (in fact, better, because you get bigger numbers, I would say) as that seen in, say, the Galápagos Islands on the equator.

6 PINKFOOTED GEESE

SNETTISHAM RSPB RESERVE

Family friendly ★
It's cold, often windy and unforgiving on the North Norfolk coast in the winter

Budget friendly ★★★★★
The cost in 2017 for a guided walk was £17 (£15 for RSPB members), and that included a full English breakfast

Amateur friendly ★★★★★
Impossible to miss the geese flying overhead

Best time of year
Mid-November-mid-January (they are present from Sept-March)

I was standing around in the half-darkness, making notes on my phone and wondering if and when the action would begin, when what sounded at first like a low hum made me look up. In the lightening gloom, it was as if a small army was coming my way, and despite the slow and steady wingbeats, it was doing so at a terrific pace.

In seconds, the birds were upon me, flying above my head, making a noise that sounded like a thousand bicycle horns. A Twitter correspondent later told they used to say the noise was like 'the rush hour in Tiananmen Square [but] the car has put paid to that analogy'. Most people refer to it as 'pinking'. Whatever, there must have been 200 or 300 in this first group, maybe more, and they continued unerringly, unwaveringly east towards the dawn.

I was at Snettisham, on the east side of The Wash, the vast, shallow indentation in Britain's North Sea coastline that's mostly famous for being the place where King John is supposed to have lost the crown jewels to the incoming tide. After spending the night roosting on the extensive mudflats, the geese were heading inland to feed on beet and potato tops and other harvest waste. Each morning – unless it's been especially clear, in which case they might have fed during the night – they do this in numbers approaching 50,000 in a good year.

DO IT YOURSELF

Snettisham RSPB Reserve (PE31 7RA) is just outside the village of Snettisham in North Norfolk. From the car park, it's about a 15-20 minute walk to the beach on good, well-signed paths. You pass a series of saline lagoons (old gravel pits) before emerging at the sea front. 🖰 www.rspb.org.uk/snettisham ☎ 01485 210779

The RSPB runs guided walks in December and January, but if you don't fancy doing one of those, then there are a few things you need to bear in mind. First, the best months are December through to the end of February. Second, in order to watch the geese leaving, you must be at the beach front just as it's getting light. Third, at the times of a full moon, the geese may feed during the night (if it's clear), so you won't see them leave.

Geese also roost on the mudflats at Holkham National Nature Reserve, a little way round the coast by Wells-next-the-Sea, and can be watched leaving from Bob Halls Sand in the same way as at Snettisham. It's run in partnership between the Holkham Estate (NR23 1RH) and Natural England. 🖰 www.holkham.co.uk/nature-reserve-beach/nature-reserve/introduction ☎ 01328 713111

It was a wet and windy morning – indeed, it was the onset of Storm Caroline – so visibility, even as dawn broke was poor. I could hear the geese chattering out on the flats but couldn't see them. They arrive in Norfolk in early November, fleeing the onset of the Arctic winter in Iceland where they breed, so despite the semi-polar conditions here, this must have felt balmy to

them. Soon, they were coming over in waves, groups ranging in size from a couple of hundred to some consisting of just two or three.

By 8.30 or so (I got there about 7), it seemed that most of the geese had departed for the day, and as a particularly torrid squall hit the coast, I beat a retreat. But I had another day in the area, so I came back the next morning, which was even colder but clear. This time, there was no problem seeing the geese massed on the mudflats and, this time, as they flew over, some of them headed straight into the orange patch of sky where the sun was starting to rise. It may sound like a clichéd image, but the sight of hundreds of geese silhouetted against the dawn sky isn't half bad on a cold winter's morning.

This time, when it was all over, I looked out into the estuary, and noticed that the tide had pushed right up against the shingle beach. I wasn't expecting this and, fixing my binoculars on the waders out on the flats, I realised that something was afoot. Suddenly, thousands of birds lifted *en masse* – mainly small wading birds called knot – and they shifted as one, this way and that, like a mass of iron filings being moved by a magnet.

They weren't as tightly packed together as starlings (**Experience 11**), so the shapes they created were not quite as vivid and never quite transcended the fact they *were* birds. Still, it was a remarkable display, and I noticed one or two

other people who had braved the frigid temperatures to watch the geese and were equally transfixed.

As I was leaving, I passed a lady who I suspected was here on a regular basis. 'Beautiful morning,' she remarked. 'Shame about the wind.' I'd barely noticed it during the past hour, but yes it was sort of blowy. Time to head back inland and get something to eat – just like the geese.

5 MINKE WHALES

STAITHES

Family friendly ★

Facilities on the boat are almost non-existent (the toilet is a bucket in the cabin), so probably not suitable for young children, and you must be able to cope with bad weather and sea swell for up to six hours

Budget friendly ★★★

For almost a day's guiding, the price is very reasonable – £90 in 2017

Amateur friendly ★★★★★

No specialist knowledge required, and you have a guide and skipper on board who are expert whale spotters

Best time of year

August-mid-Sept

What you're looking for,' said Richard Baines pointing at the sea, 'is something that isn't this. If you see something, and it's still there a moment later, then it isn't a whale. If you see something and then it's gone, report it.' We were perhaps half a mile out of Staithes, a picturesque fishing village at the edge of the North York Moors National Park, and so far, all we'd seen and heard was a cacophony of great black-backed gulls.

DO IT YOURSELF

Trips out of Staithes are run by Yorkshire Coast Nature. ☝ www.yorkshirecoastnature. co.uk ☎ 01723 865498

Whitby Whale Watching operates two boats, both out of Whitby. The ketch, Specksioneer, is recommended because the whales are said to be more attracted to it. ☝ www. whitbywhalewatching.net ☎ 07941 450381

Another location where you have a chance of seeing minke whales is around the Inner and Outer Hebrides. Try Hebridean Whale Cruises. ☝ www.hebridean-whale-cruises.co.uk ☎ 01445 712 458

In Britain, whales are even more unpredictable than other wildlife, so there's a good chance we wouldn't see one. Or if we did, it would be a fleeting glimpse and then gone. What wouldn't happen was two and a half hours of unbroken entertainment as seven minke whales surrounded us and partied. That was out of the question.

Minke whales are the smallest of the baleen whales – the group that lives by filter-feeding and also includes blues and humpbacks – growing up to a maximum of 10 metres long. They are found in cold waters, both north and south of the equator, and are (along with sperm whales) the commonest of the so-called great whales. Generally speaking, if you want to see whales, you either have to go to somewhere very cold like Antarctica or Iceland, or somewhere very warm like Baja California or the Azores.

The North Sea, off East Yorkshire from July to October, is a surprisingly good substitute for these places, however. For two months of the year, minke whales come here to feed on the substantial herring shoals that spawn on the seabed. Opinions differ as to whether this is a new phenomenon, or whether

they've always done it and nobody noticed, but whatever the truth, it's only since 2013 that a nascent whale-watching industry has begun to flourish.

I joined a small, 7 or 8 metre fishing boat skippered by Sean Baxter, while Richard, who runs other wildlife tours for his company, Yorkshire Coast Nature, was our guide. I'd come with my partner, Louise, who had never seen a whale before, and while I hadn't quite promised her one, this was a rare weekend away without our children, so there was a lot riding on it. We were lucky that the day dawned sunny, bright, and not too windy, because it would make it easier to spot anything among the swell.

Leaving Staithes, we were soon seeing guillemots, razorbills and even a solitary juvenile puffin that ought to have been far out in the North Atlantic by now and looked strangely un-puffin-like because its bill had none of the bright breeding colours you normally see. A gannet soared by on its huge 2-metre wingspan, and then – nothing.

I was just beginning to get a bad feeling about it, when there was a shout from Richard. 'Whale!' he screeched, the pure and visceral excitement of the encounter evident in his voice, even though he's seen dozens over the years. That's the thing about whales – they almost force you to feel happy.

For a minute or two, I saw nothing, and I was just starting to think that woud be it, when the whale surfaced again, some 10 metres away. Its huge, glistening black back broke the surface of the water and moved through an arc in slow-motion as if being rotated by an invisible spindle. Despite this, taking photos of it was like trying to nail down jelly.

After that, it was constant activity for the next two and a half hours. Skipper Sean used the ultrasound device in his tiny cabin to position us above the spawning herring, then cut the engine and just let us drift. All of us were now in a state of high alert, completely immersed in what we were doing, and (it felt to me) an unofficial competition started to develop as to who could see the next minke whale to surface first.

'11 o'clock!'

'Straight ahead, about 30 metres away!'

Or in my case, just a frantic, 'There!' as a sleek back and hooked dorsal fin – bigger than I'd expected – briefly exited their watery domain. When they exhaled close to the boat, there was an odour of boiled cabbage, and when they dived, they left calm patches on the water – whale footprints – that remained visible for several minutes.

There was a recognisably much smaller whale, a calf with its parent, which Richard and Sean reckoned they'd seen before. When a small skein of red-throated divers winged its way past, nobody acknowledged it. 'Only minke whales good enough for you now,' said Sean sarcastically. Well, sorry, yes.

4   NIGHTINGALES AT MIDNIGHT

HIGHNAM WOODS RSPB RESERVE

Family friendly ★★
Probably not one for young children or teens (unless they are very keen)

Budget friendly ★★★★★
Even a guided walk is excellent value – going on your own is free

Amateur friendly ★★★★
Nightingales can be heard from the carpark, but to get the full experience, you'll need to wander rough tracks in the dark

Best time of year
The last week of April until the end of May

It was a still, moonlit night on a Wednesday in mid-May, and at 11pm – while the children slept and my partner was preparing to turn in – I grabbed a thermos of hot chocolate, a warm coat and a hat and headed out the door. Half an hour later, I pulled into the carpark of Highnam Woods, just off the A40 a few miles west of Gloucester. I got out of the car, and somewhere nearby, in the moonlight, a bird was singing.

It was a song that was hard to define. Sometimes the notes were long and pure and liquid, as if they had drooled out of its mouth like honey dripping off a spoon, and next they came out all chitter-chatter but with a distinctly electronic feel, like a machine gun played through a synthesiser. The occasional car or lorry rumbled past on the main road, but the bird had no intention of stopping. In the words of that lesser musical genius Lionel Richie, this bird was going to 'sing along / All night long.'

I am no expert on nightingales, and until that night, I could count on the fingers of one hand the number of times I'd heard them, but I knew, absolutely, that this was one. No other British songbird sings like this in the dead of night. It couldn't be anything else.

As the nature writer Mark Cocker points out in *Birds Britannica*, nightingales have inspired 'a greater body of poetry in the English language than any

DO IT YOURSELF

Highnam Woods (GL2 8AA) is easy to find – the car park is located just off the A40 a few miles west of Gloucester. If heading from Gloucester to Ross-on-Wye, it's just after the turning to Newent and the village of Highnam itself, opposite the petrol station. The carpark is likely to be closed at night, unless you've made a prior arrangement with the RSPB. ✍ www.rspb.org/highnamwoods ☎ 01594 562852

In Britain, nightingales are only found in the south of England (draw a line from The Wash to the Severn Estuary to see where their range is). The RSPB runs a National Nightingale Festival every year – click on the 'Reserves and Events' tab on the website's home page to find out more.

Other good locations include: Grafham Water (PE28 0GW) and Paxton Pits (PE19 6ET) in Cambridgeshire; Fingringhoe in Essex; Minsmere (IP17 3BY) in Suffolk; Pagham Harbour and Knepp Castle Estate (RH13 8LJ) in Sussex; Blean Woods (CT2 9DD) and Northward Hill (ME3 8DS) in Kent; and Cotswold Water Park in Gloucestershire.

For Cotswold Water Park, contact CWP Trust about guided walks they offer. ✍ www.waterpark.org/cwp-trust ☎ 01793 752413

other species', with Keats' *Ode to a Nightingale* merely the most famous. 'When nightingales hold forth, notions like art or conscious invention – ideas that seem at the heart of our own definition as human beings – hover dangerously in the air,' Cocker declares.

Well, there may be something in that, I'm not sure. What I do know is that listening to these birds, which can create 250 musical phrases from an ingredients' list that numbers an estimated 600 separate notes, holding forth in darkness was like nothing else I'd ever experienced. With warden Hannah Booth, I did a tour of the woods (they're not big), and in just 45 minutes we – I should say, she – counted 11 individual singing males.

They're not visible at the best of times – unlike songbirds such as thrushes or blackbirds, which frequently declaim from the highest perch of a tall tree, nightingales announce their presence to rivals by jumping into the nearest thicket. In the half darkness, I heard birds that were singing their hearts out just a few metres away, and I could barely see the person who was standing next to me.

As with many birds, the song has a dual purpose – it's both to attract a female and to warn any rival males that they have staked a claim to the territory in which they're singing. They're migrants, so they only come here to breed, flying over from West Africa to spend a few short months of the spring and summer with us.

The earliest arrivals touch down on UK territory around mid-April, and the males immediately set about establishing their territories in the best possible locations. They can sing at almost any time of day, though early morning, late afternoon into early evening and then the night itself are the most reliable times. Many nightingales take a short breather of a couple of hours or so around 7.30 in the evening, not starting up again until 9.30, Hannah told me, but they can sing for many hours a day.

It's thought that once a male has bagged a female, he stops singing, but no one knows for sure. What is true is that once she has laid her eggs, he plays no part in bringing up the chicks. By mid-July, they've gone, having spent just three months here.

'Three months of the year?' I remarked to Hannah, 'It hardly seems worth it.'

'Oh, I don't know,' she replied.

3 GREY SEAL PUPS

BLAKENEY POINT, NORTH NORFOLK

Family friendly ★★

Amazing close encounters of
the seal kind – but bear in mind,
Blakeney Point is a wild and
weather-lashed location in the
winter

Budget friendly ★★★★

Yes, if you walk along the
point – even the boat trip is not
expensive

Amateur friendly ★★★★★

Hard not to recognise a seal –
but mind how you go, both for
your sake and theirs

Best time of year:

Nov-Dec

Toilets (in Cley next the Sea) ✓
Cafe (in Cley next the Sea) ✓

The female was having none of it. In no
uncertain terms, she told the large male
with his bulbous snout to BACK OFF
and leave her and her vulnerable pup – still
with its white coat, just a week or two old –
alone. He thought about it for a few seconds,
and then did as she said. Peace was restored,
though the female was sporting a bloody patch around her left eye, the result,
I'm guessing, of an earlier clash.

The male was probably not a threat to her pup (infanticide – where males
deliberately kill and even eat the pups – has been shown to happen in grey
seals, though it's not common), but he certainly wanted to mate with her if
he could. It's a strange quirk of their biology that females are fertile almost
immediately after giving birth.

It wasn't just the behaviour of the seals that was wild here. Blakeney Point
is an exposed spit of quite steeply shelving shingle on Norfolk's north coast,
and where I was standing all I could see was the cold grey sea stretching out
into the December mist, the shingle itself and seals. There was no one else
around. Both the location and the weather gave me a sense of isolation that

DO IT YOURSELF

Blakeney Point is a shingle spit some 4km long that runs east to west along Norfolk's north coast and harbours saltmarsh on its southern side. It's one of Britain's largest grey seal colonies, and every year an estimated 2,000 pups are born here. It's a National Nature Reserve but is owned and managed by the National Trust. ⌖ www.nationaltrust.org.uk/blakeney-national-nature-reserve ☎ 01263 740241

You can walk out along the point, but during the breeding season, some of it is out-of-bounds to the public to protect the seals from disturbance. You'll still encounter many seals (and their pups) that are not within this cordoned-off area. Treat them with respect, and never get too close. If they shows signs of distress, back away. The National Trust has special advice for people wanting to walk out to the colony. ⌖ www.nationaltrust.org.uk/blakeney-national-nature-reserve/features/responsible-seal-viewing

Access the point from Cley next the Sea Beach (NR25 7RZ). You can get very close to the seals by taking a boat trip, either with Beans Boats (⌖ www.beansboattrips.co.uk ☎ 01263 740505) or Temples Seal Trips (⌖ www.sealtrips.co.uk ☎ 01263 740791). All trips leave from Morston Quay (NR25 7BH), just outside of the village of Blakeney, where there's a National Trust car park (free to members).

There are plenty of other locations in Britain where you can see grey seals – for example, Coquet Island (Experience 38) off the coast of Northumberland, Bardsey Island (Experience 70), off the coast of North Wales, much of the coast of Pembrokeshire, including Skomer (Experience 22) and Ramsey Island.

Boat trips to and around Ramsey are a great way to see them. Trips are provided by Voyages of Discovery (⌖ www.ramseyisland.co.uk ☎ 0800 854 367) and Thousand Island Expeditions (⌖ thousandislands.co.uk ☎ 01437 721721).

is rare in England, and together with the testosterone-charged male and his (so-far) unwilling mate, I felt like I could have been somewhere like South Georgia in the South Atlantic, not East Anglia.

And there were loads of seals here. Some of the point is out-of-bounds to the public during pupping season – roughly November through to January – but I was way outside that no-go zone, and there were little family groups all around me. I had to be careful not to disturb them – the biggest threat to the pups is if they get caught and accidentally crushed by a fight between two adults, so you really don't want to set off a commotion, and I didn't want to be on the receiving end of a bite from one of those males.

I'd walked about 3km from the car park at Cley next the Sea beach, and there had been plenty to ponder on the way – a whitecoat pup on its own that, if it had been abandoned by its mother for any reason, was

doomed, and later a dead one, untouched apart from its eyeballs that had been plucked by a hungry gull. As I walked along the beach, male seals were swimming up and down just metres away, watching me carefully as they patrolled their territory, making sure I moved on, like a dog in a South American village routing vehicles as they pass through. They were as lithe and athletic in the water as they were awkward out of it – the way a seal moves on land reminds me of an especially cumbersome caterpillar.

At one point, I was hit by a vicious squall, a combination of wind and sleety rain that came from nowhere. I turned my back and waited, hoping it wouldn't last too long – there was no shelter anywhere within miles – just me, the point, the cold grey sea and the seals.

2 SWIMMING WITH BASKING SHARKS

COLL, INNER HEBRIDES

Family friendly ★
Not suitable for children or anyone who isn't a competent swimmer or snorkeler

Amateur friendly ★★★
No specialist knowledge needed, but previous snorkelling experience essential

Budget friendly ★
Finding basking sharks is a complex operation, and the costs are consequently high

Best time of year
mid-July to early Sept

It was a bright and breezy day in early September, and I was sitting on the side of a boat in the middle of Gunna Sound, between the Inner Hebridean islands of Coll and Tiree. My feet were dangling over the sides of the deck, and for the umpteenth

DO IT YOURSELF

Basking sharks can grow up to 10m long but are harmless to humans because they feed on plankton. They are found in temperate waters in both the northern and southern hemispheres and are named for their habit of 'basking' at the surface.

The best place to see basking sharks in Britain is between the islands of Coll and Tiree in the Inner Hebrides from the last week of July until early/mid-September. Scientists believe they gather here to mate and feed, though nothing is known for certain.

Basking Shark Scotland (BSS) is the only operator running dedicated basking shark trips in which you can snorkel with them. Finding basking sharks – unless it's calm – is difficult, and success is not guaranteed. BSS can provide all the necessary snorkelling equipment you'll need (including the wetsuits, fins etc). It does 1-4 day trips, which cost from about £200-700. ⌂ baskingsharkscotland. co.uk ☎ 07975 723140

You will need to find your own way to Coll. Ferries leave from Oban on Scotland's west coast. Caledonian MacBrayne ⌂ www.calmac.co.uk ☎ 0800 066 5000

Finding long-stay parking in Oban can be tricky. The best option I found was the one on Shore Street, which (2017) costs £5 a day and is about a five-minute walk from the ferry terminal.

There are a number of operators that run trips off the South Coast, but basking sharks are less numerous here and encounters less reliable. Charles Hood Photography ⌂ charleshood. com ☎ 07712 622420; Atlantic Diving ⌂ atlanticdiver.co.uk ☎ 01637 850930; and Porthkerris Divers ⌂ porthkerris.com ☎ 01326 280620

You can also see basking sharks off the Isle of Man. See Manx Basking Shark Watch for more information. ⌂ www.manxbaskingsharkwatch.org/news/boat-trips

time, I spat in my mask and leant over to wash it out with sea water. The truth is, I was feeling rather nervous.

'Of course I won't get swallowed by one,' was the last thing I said to my family as I set off on a madcap, overnight drive north to Oban, with a whole two hours' sleep in a Travelodge at Dumbarton, before catching the 5.15am ferry to Coll. 'Or get whacked by its tail.' But now that I was about to get into the water with the world's second largest shark, I was suddenly reflecting that I was no Jacques Cousteau, so if one of these beasts did come straight towards me, I wasn't certain I'd know how to react.

Our guides, Tammy and Inga, had already given us very thorough instructions on what to do and when to do it, or we'd miss seeing the shark. 'When we say look down,' Inga said, 'make sure you look down.' Then came the order – the shark was coming towards us.

I plunged into the choppy waters, and was pleasantly surprised by how warm it was (but then, I was wearing an 8mm wetsuit with boots, flippers, gloves and hood) and how easily I floated, but now I was in the water, there was no way of telling where the shark was. Cameron, the boat skipper, had positioned us in its expected path, and – any moment now – it was due to swim right past. On board the boat, Inga was tracking its dorsal fin and shouting instructions to Tammy.

'OK, look down,' Tammy said, 'It's coming.' I looked down, and was momentarily distracted by a large, beautiful but slightly sinister lion's mane jellyfish floating some 10 feet below me. Nice, but not what I'd driven 500 miles for, so I quickly looked up and across.

Almost immediately, the shark loomed out of the milky water. It was so close, I felt as if I could have reached out and touched it, and slightly to my surprise, it looked exactly like a basking shark should. It hadn't got its cavernous mouth open (so, phew, there's went any possibility of getting swallowed) and it was barely moving that massive tail (I wouldn't get whacked, either).

The visibility in the water was poor, but because the sun was shining at this precise moment, the shark was illuminated as it swam past so that I felt I could see every indentation on rough skin the colour of a rhino's. Its left eye was looking straight at me, but I doubt I registered on the beast's consciousness. The five massive gill slits just behind its head left me in no doubt that this was, indeed, a fish. It was almost hyper-real, reminding me of a back-lit photo at the annual Wildlife Photographer of the Year competition in the Natural History Museum.

The shark came and went in about 10 seconds and that was the last we saw of it. We spent another hour looking for more sharks (this was our third encounter of the morning, but the only time we managed to get into the water with one), but the wind was increasing, and Cameron eventually decided we needed to get across to the sheltered side of Mull before we were stuck on Coll by the storm.

But despite the brevity, it was an extraordinary encounter – a moment in time, perfectly framed, come and gone in seconds, but etched fiercely into my memory bank.

1 FISHING WHITE-TAILED EAGLES

LOCH NA KEAL, ISLE OF MULL

Family friendly ★★★★★
Suitable for children at least as young as 3 or 4

Budget friendly ★★★
A family of four (with children under 14) will pay £130 (2017 prices) for a three-hour trip, but it's worth every penny

Amateur friendly ★★★★★
You don't need any specialist knowledge to appreciate white-tailed eagles

Best time of year
April-Oct

Toilets (on the boat) ✓

'The big bird is coming,' my son, Mungo, said in an alarmed and rising tone. 'The big bird is coming.'

He wasn't wrong. He was three and a half at the time, and the bird in question – a white tailed eagle – has a wing span of at least two metres, and a body length of nearly a metre. My son was also about a metre tall, but his wingspan was half that of the eagle's. No wonder he thought the bird was big – it probably looked twice his size.

It was flying towards our boat across the water of Loch Na Keal, its eyes fixed on the dead fish that skipper Martin Keivers had just thrown out from the stern. As it drew nearer, the eagle glided down on still wings until its talons were poised inches above the water, and then it plucked the fish from the surface and flew off to the far shore where it could eat its prize in peace.

If you look up, you can see white-tailed eagles almost everywhere on Mull. There are 21 pairs spread over most of the island, and these days, they are both its (and, really, the UK's) top land predator. Since we lost wolves, lynx and bears over the past two millennia, there is really nothing that can compete with eagles.

This is a rare British conservation success story. So many of our species are in trouble thanks to loss of habitat or, in the case of birds of prey, persecution, but white-tailed eagles have come back from extinction thanks to a far-sighted

DO IT YOURSELF

Mull Charters is the only operation on Mull that offers trips to see white-tailed eagles fishing. ☝ www.mullcharters.com ☎ 01680 300444 or 07788 677131. Trips leave from the community-built jetty at Ulva Ferry on the west side of Mull.

The Mull Eagle Watch project offers guided white-tailed eagle walks – locations may vary from year to year, but they are great value and the RSPB and community rangers are superb guides. Booking necessary with VisitScotland. ☝ www.mulleaglewatch.com ☎ 01680 812556

Other good locations for white-tailed eagles include: Rum, Wester Ross (just north of the Isle of Skye) and the Outer Hebrides, especially Harris and Lewis, though none of these are as good as Mull. They can also be seen on the east coast of Scotland, particularly in Fife (the part of Scotland sandwiched between the Firth of Forth and the River Tay), where there was a reintroduction programme between 2007 and 2012. Loch Leven is a good place to start in this part of the world.

Some Scottish-based operators offer extended tours that will give you an excellent chance to see white-tailed eagles – they include Heatherlea (☝ www.heatherlea.co.uk ☎ 01479 821248) and Speyside Wildlife (☝ www.speysidewildlife.co.uk ☎ 01479 812498)

FISHING WHITE-TAILED EAGLES

reintroduction programme that began in the 1975. The reintroductions were actually first carried out on Rum some 30km to the north, but they've done better on Mull, which is now the white-tailed eagle capital of Britain.

Our eagle only returned for his free meal once more, but two adrenaline-pumping, heart-stopping close encounters (of the bird kind) were quite sufficient. And it wasn't our only sighting of these flying monsters. Earlier in the week, Dave Sexton of the RSPB took us to a viewpoint from where he trained his spotting scope on a nest some 70 or 80 metres away. A juvenile eagle, fully grown but still reliant on the food bank of mum and dad, was perched beside it, waiting perhaps for one of its parents to return with the shopping.

My other, then six-year-old son, Sam, was amazed to see the bird suddenly shoot out a remarkably bright, white defecation that was visible, even from this distance, with the naked eye and burst out laughing. Even deadly predators have to go to the bathroom, and it's become a family story that he still enjoys being retold three years later.

We saw them, too, on a cycle ride (we cheated and hired electric bikes in Salen) around Loch Na Keal, a much better way of getting around if you want almost any kind of wildlife sightings. In this case, it was the throaty cronk of a raven that

alerted us to the eagle's presence (which we wouldn't have heard if we'd been driving in a car), and we watched as a couple of these corvids – which are the size of buzzards themselves – mobbed the intruder.

But, in my view, nothing quite compares with seeing a white-tailed eagle slowly descending to the surface of a loch, undercarriage extended, its focus entirely on the business of bringing home the bacon. Mungo certainly thought so.

INDEX

100 GREAT WILDLIFE EXPERIENCES